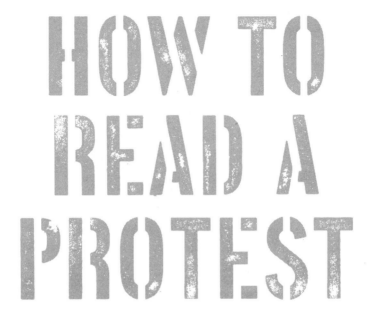

HOW TO READ A PROTEST

HOW TO READ A PROTEST

THE ART OF ORGANIZING AND RESISTANCE

L. A. KAUFFMAN

UNIVERSITY OF CALIFORNIA PRESS

University of California Press, one of the most distinguished university presses in the United States, enriches lives around the world by advancing scholarship in the humanities, social sciences, and natural sciences. Its activities are supported by the UC Press Foundation and by philanthropic contributions from individuals and institutions. For more information, visit www.ucpress.edu.

University of California Press
Oakland, California

Designer: Lia Tjandra
Compositor: Lia Tjandra and IDS Infotech Limited
Printer: Maple Press

Library of Congress Cataloging-in-Publication Data

Names: Kauffman, L.A., author.
Title: How to read a protest : the art of organizing and resistance / L.A. Kauffman.
Description: Oakland, California : University of California Press, [2018] | Includes bibliographical references and index. |
Identifiers: LCCN 2018019777 (print) | LCCN 2018024177 (ebook) | ISBN 9780520972209 (e-book) | ISBN 9780520301528 (cloth : alk. paper)
Subjects: LCSH: Protest movements—United States—History—20th century. | Protest movements—United States—History—21st century.
Classification: LCC HM883 (ebook) | LCC HM883 .K38 2018 (print) | DDC 303.48/409730904—dc23
LC record available at https://lccn.loc .gov/2018019777

Manufactured in the United States of America

26 25 24 23 22 21 20 19 18
10 9 8 7 6 5 4 3 2 1

To N. and D.

CONTENTS

HOW TO READ A PROTEST / 1

Acknowledgments / 109

A Note on Protest Numbers / 113

Notes / 115

Selected Bibliography and Recommended Reading / 127

Photo Credits / 131

Index / 135

Marchers fill Constitution Avenue during the 1963 March on Washington for Jobs and Freedom.

A crowd of marchers on Pennsylvania Avenue during the 2017 Women's March on Washington. Photo by Mario Tama

HOW TO READ A PROTEST

Protests work—just not, perhaps, the way you think.

When you're in the midst of a demonstration, especially a very large one, the sense of collective power is stirring and immediate. There's a great feeling of purpose and unity when you stand with a huge crowd of other people who share your outrage over an injustice and your eagerness for action. Joining a protest, whatever the cause, gives you the direct bodily experience of being part of something larger than yourself. In a literal and immediate way, you add your heart and your voice to a movement.

But afterward, you might wonder if that's all there is. You march, and it feels good to march, but did the marching matter? And if it did, what *exact* difference did it make? Do protests change policy? Do they change minds? Or do they just let off steam? Millions of Americans have taken to the streets in recent times, breaking previous records for protest participation, but there's widespread skepticism around demonstrations—a suspicion that protests are purely expressive, a venting of frustration with no quantifiable effect, and that the real work of reform happens through established channels of influence like elections and lobbying. Every time there's a major wave of protests in the United States, a flurry of think pieces follows, questioning whether demonstrations accomplish anything that can be measured. We celebrate past protests that we think did have lasting impact, from the stately 1963 March on Washington for Jobs and Freedom to the unruly 1969 Stonewall riots that kicked off the modern LGBTQ movement, but there's often a gestural quality to the acclaim, a broad sense that these actions helped create change, but no detailed accounting of exactly how and why.

Some protests, of course, have no more enduring effect than a gust of wind. There are failures as well as successes in any area of human endeavor, and with protests, the odds are against you from the start. By definition, people demonstrate when normal channels are blocked or unresponsive, when institutions allow injustice to flourish, when the powerful act with impunity. Protests are what political scientist and anthropologist James C. Scott famously called "weapons of the weak," used by those who lack the power to achieve their goals through official means. The ultimate measure of a movement's success may be if it can move from protest to power, from an outside critique to inside influence, but history moves slowly and unevenly. Structures of power are entrenched and resilient, and injustices go deep. The work of movements is filled with setbacks, reversals, and defeats, and victories are often partial or fragile or both. You may need many years of changing attitudes before you can begin to change policy. You may lose for a very long time before you begin to win. If power conceded without demands, protests would never be necessary.

Protests come in many forms, and happen on wildly varying scales, from a single individual kneeling on a football field to a million people marching through the streets of a major city. There are as many kinds of protests as there are tools in a well-stocked toolbox, and part of the difficulty in coming to terms with what protests do is that they don't all work in the same way. A silent vigil, say, and a freeway blockade are as different in character and effect as a sanding block and a sledgehammer. A vigil is a bid for public sympathy, an appeal to the heart and to common ground. A blockade is intentionally polarizing and controversial; in creating a logistical crisis, it seeks to create a political one, forcing those in power to respond. Successful movements tend to use many different tactics, of which protests are only the most visible, and skilled organizers will use protests of different kinds at different moments in an unfolding campaign.

The most iconic form of protest in America is the mass march, exemplified by the legendary 1963 event where Dr. Martin Luther King Jr. delivered his "I Have a Dream" speech. Mass protests may be the hardest of all to evaluate, even as they've become recurring fixtures of American political life. At first glance, they all look similar, with huge crowds converging on the nation's capital or some other major city to take a public stand. But they are not all alike. Mass protests have been organized very differently over time, and their function has varied and evolved as part of a long series of shifts in the nature of movements and activism in America. Sometimes, a huge demonstration can function like the capstone to a movement, as happened with the 1963 march, which is widely viewed as representing what a successful protest can be. On other occasions, mass protests can channel vast anger with seemingly no effect on the course of events, as happened on the eve of the Iraq War in 2003. In the hope of deterring President George W. Bush from waging a war on false pretenses, millions around the globe poured into the streets for what remains the single largest day of protest in world history; the massive outcry, however, failed to stop the Bush administration's rush to war. And, in rare and remarkable instances, a mass mobilization can help galvanize and energize a sprawling new movement, as the 2017 Women's Marches did with the resistance to Trump. These nationwide marches were organized differently from any major protests in American history, and the bottom-up, women-led way they came together gave them a powerful and unprecedented movement-building impact. If you want to understand what protests do and when and how they work, you first have to understand their character: You need to know how to read a protest.

An excellent place to begin is by looking carefully at the signs that demonstrators carry. After all, signs are often the first thing that tells you a protest is a protest and not some other large assemblage of people, like a crowd waiting to enter a performance venue or celebrating the victory of a sports team. People carry signs to communicate, and to affiliate—to tell the broader public how they feel and what they want, and to show they identify with a movement or a group. In most cases, you should be able to figure out at a glance whether a protest concerns the construction of a gas pipeline or the police murder of an unarmed Black teenager or an elected representative's vote to gut health care. Big protests, especially, almost always feature signs or banners, and these offer rich clues to what's really going on: how the demonstration came together, what kind of movement it grew out of, who sponsored it, and what impact it might have.

Take a look: Are the signs professionally printed, by and large, and quite similar in appearance? That's what the posters looked like at the most famous demonstration in US history, the 1963 March on Washington. Examine images from that day and you'll see impeccably dressed marchers carrying uniform-looking placards, each trumpeting an urgent demand: "WE DEMAND VOTING RIGHTS *NOW!*" "WE MARCH FOR INTEGRATED SCHOOLS *NOW!*" "WE MARCH FOR JOBS FOR ALL *NOW!*"

The 1963 March on Washington is so universally known and so widely celebrated that for many people it's what comes first to mind when thinking of demonstrations at all. It's the benchmark against which other large protests are most often measured, so mythic that it almost stands above and outside history in many people's imaginations—as a pinnacle moment of social struggle, in which the pressing need for change in America's racial order was conveyed with such force and dignity that reform seemed natural and inevitable. Scholars might debate how much the march can be credited with the passage of the Civil Rights Act the following year—overall, they're skeptical, seeing it as but one step in a long and complex process—but the connection is firmly cemented in popular understandings of American history. This sense that the march helped secure the passage of key civil rights legislation, along with the enduring resonance of the powerful words that King spoke from the steps of the Lincoln Memorial, have led many to view the 1963 March on Washington as the consummate example of what a successful protest can and should be: a convergence that so beautifully crystallizes and amplifies the concerns of those gathered that it pressures recalcitrant institutions to act. By any standard, the event came off splendidly, stirring the world's conscience, and more than a half century later, it continues to inspire and educate.

But much as the larger history of the civil rights movement has often been distorted and depoliticized in the retelling, so has the nature and impact of this key protest. Of course the 1963 March on Washington contributed to the multifaceted effort to pass federal civil rights legislation in the United States, but the contribution was relatively indirect. It helped create a sense of national consensus around civil rights and gave a new stature and legitimacy to the movement—that is to say, it had a diffuse and long-term influence, the very sort that tends to be either ignored or dismissed as political failure when pundits evaluate other mass protests. Political scientist Jeanne Theoharis has written powerfully about how myths of the civil rights movement have been "weaponized" against subsequent movements, setting up a hallowed standard against which all other efforts have been harshly judged. In popular discourse, a grandeur and effectiveness has been attributed to the 1963 March on Washington that no subsequent march could ever match. In sanctifying this one protest and making it larger than life, all other protests are diminished by comparison.[1]

The more closely you look at how the march was actually organized, and what impact it had on the unfolding civil rights movement, the more it stands out as singular and anomalous. In a great many respects, from the way the organizing proceeded to the effects that it had, the 1963 March on Washington was unlike any other demonstration that came before or after it. The eye-catching signs that marchers carried on that storied August afternoon are just one small detail in the great drama of the day, but they help explain what made it so unique—and in so doing, help explain how the political landscape for protest, and the parameters for what protests can and do accomplish, have shifted over the decades since. The posters at the 1963 March on Washington look so uniform for a quite

Volunteers stack signs at the DC office for the 1963 March on Washington in advance of the event.

extraordinary reason. They were completely controlled by the organizers, who took great care to make sure that the only signs that appeared at the demonstration were ones featuring slogans they had approved. So unusual was this course of action that it would never be repeated at any other sizable demonstration in the United States: The protest march that's come to epitomize peaceful popular dissent in America was an event where all but authorized messages were silenced.

To understand how and why this happened, it's crucial to remember that the 1963 March on Washington was the first event of its kind. It was not the first demonstration in the nation's capital, but it was the first genuinely mass one, and the first protest march of its size in US history. The man who would direct the organizing, longtime civil rights and labor leader A. Philip Randolph, had dreamed for decades of holding a massive march on Washington, but none had ever actually happened. There had been a few noteworthy prior events in DC that were designed to showcase collective strength, but they were modest in scale and almost always parade-like in character. Five thousand women marched along Pennsylvania Avenue, for instance, for an elaborate 1913 Suffrage Procession and Pageant. A little more than a decade later, the Ku Klux Klan, then just past the peak of its popularity, brought 50,000 of its members to parade through Washington in full hooded regalia in 1925 and 1926. Some 17,000 World War I veterans came to demand their bonus pay in 1932, in the one sizable pre-1963 DC protest that wasn't organized in parade fashion; the Bonus Army's ragged occupation ended in bloodshed after President Hoover ordered the police to evict them. A. Philip Randolph had announced a major march in 1941 to protest racial segregation in the armed forces, an all-Black mobilization that he vowed would top 100,000 attendees, but he called it off at the last minute after then-President Roosevelt met the protest's central demand and signed an executive order prohibiting racial discrimination in federal training programs and defense industries. Until the 1963 event that we've come to think of as the basic template for big national protests, there was, in fact, just one mass protest march of any kind in America, a beautifully organized civil rights demonstration by more than 125,000 people in Detroit that took place in late June 1963, when work on the

Women's Suffrage Parade proceeds down Pennsylvania Avenue, 1913.

March on Washington was just getting under way. The success of this little-remembered event, the Detroit Walk to Freedom, helped spur and solidify plans for the DC march.[2]

So the planning for the 1963 March on Washington has to be understood as brand-new and unprecedented, a bold and audacious experiment with a type of collective action that hadn't been tried in the United States before. "Mobilization" is first and foremost a military term—the readying

Members of the Ku Klux Klan parade on Pennsylvania Avenue, ca. 1926.

and amassing of troops for war—and before that August Wednesday, no civilian force in the United States had ever tried to move people on this scale for political purposes. There had been very large parades of various kinds, from ticker tape parades celebrating distinguished foreign visitors or victorious sports teams to the famous Macy's Thanksgiving Day Parade, which dates back to the 1920s, but the huge crowds who attended these events came as spectators, not as marchers. To a substantial degree, organizing the March on Washington was a matter of improvisation and guesswork, as there were no prior models to follow for organizing a protest this large. And although the staff and coalition for the event included significant white participation, it's worth stressing that the mass protest march in America was fundamentally a Black invention: conceived of by Black leaders, shaped by Black organizing traditions, and mostly built through Black organizations and networks. Preliminary political discussions about the march began many months ahead of time, but the logistics for this enormous undertaking were largely thrown together in a dizzying eight weeks. Randolph was the official director, but his deputy, the legendary organizer Bayard Rustin, whose homosexuality and past ties to the Communist Party made him too controversial to serve as the acknowledged leader, served as the hands-on coordinator for the endeavor.

Six civil rights organizations, of varying strength and character, came together to cosponsor the march. Their leaders, the so-called Big Six, constituted the decision-making body for the march, which was later expanded to include the heads of the United Auto Workers and major Protestant, Catholic, and Jewish organizations, who together were called the Big Ten. A somewhat larger administrative committee was tasked with implementation. All six groups donated staff members and other resources to the effort, and to different degrees leveraged their mailing lists and networks of local contacts to recruit participants. Randolph's organization, the little-known Negro American Labor Council (NALC), kicked off the initial work. The Student Nonviolent Coordinating Committee (SNCC) and the Congress of Racial Equality (CORE), two groups that favored bold direct action and innovative local organizing to challenge racial segregation, came on board early, but both groups' enthusiasm for the march waned as the planning proceeded and its character grew ever milder and more orchestrated. Some local CORE chapters were quite active in publicizing the march and mobilizing people to come, but others openly criticized the

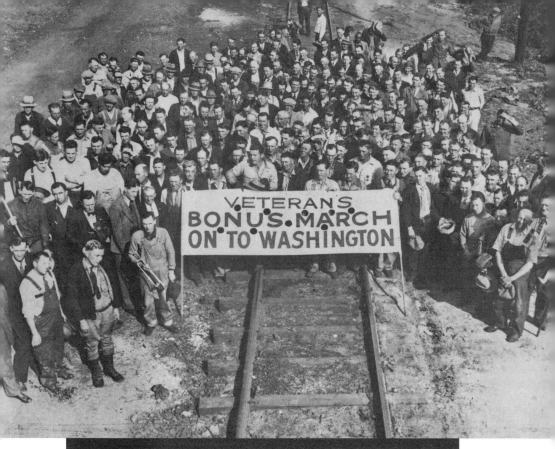

Bonus Army marchers from Oregon en route to Washington, DC, to demand their pay, 1932.

event as too tame and compromised. Dr. King's organization, the Southern Christian Leadership Conference (SCLC), brought moral authority and of course the charismatic and inspiring figure of King himself, as well as a network of clergy whom organizers hoped would mobilize their flocks—the march was scheduled for a Wednesday specifically so pastors would be free to bring their congregations. The SCLC, though, did not typically have strong local infrastructure—within the wider civil rights movement, King and his organization were often faulted for parachuting into sites of local conflict only to depart when the spotlight waned—and it was so financially and organizationally strapped that it contributed little money or mobilizing might to the effort. The august National Association for the Advancement of Colored People (NAACP) had the biggest membership and strongest network of local chapters of all the groups that came together for the march, and its infrastructure proved crucial to bringing the huge crowds to Washington. The NAACP's long-standing preference for legal and legislative work and caution around street protests, however, meant that it would participate only if Randolph and Rustin agreed to scrap any plans for civil disobedience and soften any radical edge to the event, which in turn blunted the enthusiasm of SNCC and CORE. The final member of the coalition, the National Urban League, had almost no experience with demonstrations, but it had other resources to contribute, from staff members to office space.[3]

Bringing these six disparate groups together to organize an event on such a grand scale required many compromises; working with the authorities in Washington, DC, entailed many more. To a degree that would never be repeated in subsequent mass national demonstrations, the planning developed in uneasy but close collaboration with one of the movement's major targets: the administration of President John F. Kennedy, whose actions in defense of the basic rights of African Americans had been limited and tepid. The shocking events in Birmingham that May, where police led by sheriff Eugene "Bull" Connor had infamously attacked civil rights protesters, including children, with police dogs and fire hoses, had finally pushed the president to introduce civil rights legislation in Congress. But

Civil rights leaders visit the White House to discuss march plans, June 22, 1963. Martin Luther King Jr. and Roy Wilkins of the NAACP are flanking Attorney General Robert F. Kennedy; lead march organizer A. Philip Randolph is barely visible at the far right.

that didn't mean Kennedy welcomed having crowds of protesters march on Washington to make sure it became law. Indeed, Kennedy did everything in his power to try to dissuade the organizers from holding the march, arguing that it would be counterproductive. "The Negroes are already in the streets," Randolph had defiantly countered at a June 22 White House meeting between civil rights leaders and the president. "There *will* be a march." For the administration, the question quickly became how to contain it, and Kennedy reportedly declared in private, "Well, if we can't stop it, we'll run the damn thing." That was a gross exaggeration of what happened, if indeed Kennedy said it at all, but there was in fact thoroughgoing coordination between protest planners and the White House on nearly every aspect of the day, going well beyond the kind of logistical support that would become standard administrative practice for protests in the future. Inevitably, this cooperation came with many subtle and not-so-subtle moves to control and limit the march, all justified on the grounds of ensuring that the event would not descend into chaos.[4]

Kennedy set the tone in July, with a statement of public support for the march that spent far more time sternly lecturing those who planned to join the event than it did affirming their aims. Despite citing "every evidence that it's going to be peaceful," Kennedy declared, "I have warned about demonstrations which could lead to riots, demonstrations which could lead to bloodshed, and I warn now again about them." He continued, "I would suggest that we exercise great care in protesting so it doesn't become riots." Of course, nearly all the violence associated with the civil rights movement as of 1963 was white violence directed toward it, and Kennedy knew that; there was a cynicism to his finger-wagging tone. As Bayard Rustin and a young march staffer, Tom Kahn, put it in a private memo to Randolph a week before the march, "It is not our people who invented lynching, who have set vicious dogs loose in the streets, who have turned high-power hoses on defenseless women and children. We have not burned buses or led insurrections against federal marshals." Nor, of course, had civil rights activists murdered their opponents, while the cold-blooded killing of NAACP official Medgar Evers on June 12 of that summer foreshadowed many assassinations to come. But the threat to marchers was not the Kennedy administration's chief concern. Indeed, just a week before Kennedy made his cautionary remarks, an official from his Justice Department had flatly refused in a meeting with Rustin and other organizers to take any action whatsoever to protect those coming to Washington from possible attacks. ("We have no legal authority to police the channels of commerce or to take any preventative action," the official blandly declared.) Lacking any guarantee that marchers would be protected from white violence—some were in fact viciously assaulted on their way home—while having to respond constantly to white fears, Rustin and Kahn's memo to Randolph concluded, "The question of violence seems to have exercised a fascination far out of proportion to what it deserves. There is no doubt but that for some people the source of this fascination is a conception that any large gathering of Negroes represents a threat of violence."[5]

That conception shaped news report after news report in the lead-up to the march, helping create an atmosphere of apprehension and anxiety. "There are a great many people, as I am sure you know, who believe that it would be impossible to bring more than 100,000 militant Negroes into Washington without incidents and possibly rioting," the host of "Meet the Press" intoned portentously in an interview with NAACP executive secretary Roy Wilkins a few days beforehand. The *Los Angeles Times* echoed this concern: "The specter of riot hangs over the march. Some 200,000 angry people in one place on a hot day in August makes for a combustible situation." This drumbeat of dire warnings was so loud and insistent that it almost seemed like some of the people issuing them hoped that things would go awry. Indeed, one Dixiecrat from Louisiana, Senator Russell B. Long, confessed, "I would just as soon the whole thing broke out in riots, though I am not advocating this. I suppose the whole South would just as soon it got out of hand." As *Life* magazine editorialized the week before

Protesters form a moving picket line outside segregated Southside Sundry in Farmville, Virginia, July 1963.

Protesters block the road leading to Jones Beach, New York, in a protest against hiring discrimination, July 1963.

the march, "It boils down to a feeling that the Negro is 'going too far.' In a recent Gallup poll six out of 10 whites felt that Negroes are hurting their own cause with undue militancy."[6]

The planning for the march was taking place, it must be said, against the backdrop of a powerful surge of local organizing, and conflict, around civil rights. Though it's not much remembered except among scholars, the summer of 1963 witnessed an extraordinary number of local civil rights protests all around the country: more than 1,100, in some 220 cities, spread throughout every region of the United States. The struggle in Birmingham had the highest profile, but it was only one of a great many flash points all around the country,

Members of CORE hold a sit-in at Southwood Homes Sales Office in Torrance, California, June 1963.

from Denver to Philadelphia to Tallahassee. In community after community, local people were using direct action, including pickets, sit-ins, and marches, to confront segregation and discrimination right where it was happening, directly placing their bodies in the way of injustice. Demonstrations took place all summer long not only at segregated lunch counters and restaurants, but also at schools, housing developments, job sites, and places of recreation such as movie theaters and swimming pools. Hundreds were arrested after protesting outside a segregated Holiday Inn in Savannah, Georgia, and outside a whites-only amusement park in Gwynn Oak, Maryland. In Long Island, protesters blocked roads leading to Jones Beach to challenge discriminatory hiring practices there; in Southern California, they occupied the sales office of a housing development to combat bias; in St. Louis, they blocked school buses that were, taking children to segregated schools. Then as now, these kinds of targeted and very direct actions were often successful at pressuring individual businesses or institutions to change, and the threat of facing such protests led numerous others to follow suit. As the *Kiplinger Washington Letter* put it in its weekly update to business leaders in late July, "Southern businessmen are reacting to the pressure in this way: Many are going along reluctantly with removal of symbols of prejudice . . . desegregating rest rooms, water fountains, lunch counters, restaurants. Hotel men say: 'Where it has been done quietly, desegregation has made little disturbance. But if we wait for trouble, sit-ins, etc. it usually means economic loss. We hope to avoid demonstrations.'" But for all the effectiveness of these local protests, they were small-scale and piecemeal by definition; the victories were tiny in comparison to the pervasiveness of discrimination. Each local advance pointed the way toward the sweeping, national policy changes that would be needed to uproot segregation, but also underscored that local action alone was insufficient.[7]

Backlash, meanwhile, was also growing, as was frustration with the slow pace of reform. At numerous local protests, demonstrators encountered violent responses from police or hostile white crowds or both,

Police remove protesters from a sit-in at segregated Gwynn Oak Amusement Park, Maryland, July 1963. Photo by Walter McCardell

as for instance in Lexington, North Carolina, where a thousand white people rioted after fifteen Black protesters tried to integrate a local bowling alley and other businesses. White racists instigated most of the clashes, but in some cases, including in Birmingham, protesters fought back by throwing bottles or rocks. As protests flared up all around the country that summer, there was an unmistakable sense that many Black communities were becoming thoroughly fed up with ongoing white intransigence. There were signs of a new militancy emerging at the grassroots in some locales, and the early stirrings of what would become Black Power. A few protests did become direct clashes, including in Cambridge, Maryland, an Eastern Shore community where local activists had been trying for some time to desegregate local restaurants and recreational facilities. The movement there, led by the poised and uncompromising Gloria Richardson, was one of the first to question strict nonviolence and embrace notions of radical self-defense, including armed self-defense. Several protests in June became so violent that martial law was declared and the National Guard brought in, developments that were in the forefront of President Kennedy's mind when he issued his cautions about the March on Washington. Though local chapters of the major national groups were involved in many of these community-level struggles, this wave of local protest spilled well beyond the preexisting organizational bounds of the civil rights movement. As scholar Thomas Gentile noted, many local protests "were relatively spontaneous outbursts of activism by individuals and small groups, most of whose past involvement in demonstrations were minimal. . . . There was often no single sponsor like CORE, SNCC, the NAACP or SCLC."[8]

The climate of fear surrounding the upcoming march, the desire to contain the restless energy from the grassroots, and pressure from the Kennedy administration shaped a great many decisions about the planning. Initially, the convergence was to take place on multiple days and involve a range of tactics, including civil disobedience and citizen lobbying; Rustin in particular hoped that militant nonviolence would give the entire gathering a strong and uncompromising tone. To secure the NAACP's involvement,

March on Washington organizer Bayard Rustin holds a map showing plans to accommodate the expected crowds.

those ideas were quickly scuttled in favor of a fully legal one-day march and rally. Plans to march to the Capitol were soon deemed too confrontational—the Capitol Grounds Act of 1882 made all such actions illegal, until it was struck down by a court in 1972. And Kennedy administration officials made it clear they didn't want the march going anywhere near the White House, either. So the route was shifted to take marchers from the Washington Monument to the Lincoln Memorial, two photogenic and symbolically rich locations that were, however, distant from any actual seat of power in DC. Many smaller logistical decisions also flowed from the climate of caution: Until

A sit-in blocks a downtown St. Louis street in a protest against school segregation, June 1963.

fairly late in the process, organizers discouraged people from coming to the march in private automobiles, feeling they could manage the crowds better if everyone arrived on buses and other organized mass transit. They told marchers to leave children at home, and instructed them to depart the District by sundown. DC authorities decided to close all liquor stores for the day, a rather insulting move, while President Kennedy placed thousands of troops on standby in case trouble erupted.

The fear also influenced how organizers decided to handle the protest signs, which represented the public face that protesters would show the world. Randolph and Rustin wanted to be sure that the event not only would be peaceful and orderly, but that it would *look* that way, too. At the same planning meeting with police officials where the Justice Department said it couldn't do anything to protect those coming to the event, a deputy DC police chief asked the organizers if marchers would be carrying "placards that will help inflame the opposition." Rustin had a ready reply. "The staff is proposing . . . that all placards used be made by the central committee and that no people coming in will be able to carry their placards," he explained to police. The idea presumably came from Randolph, who had intended to control all signs and slogans for the big 1941 march that was called off after it achieved its aims. The signs that marchers would carry for the 1963 event, Rustin reassured police officials, would be "designed for the maintenance of order."[9]

That was indeed how the National Committee decided to handle the signs. The first organizing manual for the march, an eight-page guide that was mailed out to local groups and organizers just a week after the police meeting, gave unambiguous instructions, underlined to emphasize their importance: "All placards to be used on the March will be provided by the National Office. No other slogans will be permitted." The organizers never publicly explained the thinking behind this decision, but the rationale clearly extended past projecting an orderly image to larger questions of political control. "The reasons for this policy should be obvious," read a passage drafted for the second organizing manual, but then cut before it went to the printer. "It would not be fair to the more than 100,000 marchers we expect if some people carried slogans which went beyond the program that formed the basis of recruitment to the March. If each of us pressed for his own program, the total impact of the March would be diffused and weakened." This was a vision of unity as unanimity, and a rather audacious level of political discipline to seek to impose on the wide array of forces that were being mobilized to attend the march. It was also a departure from standard civil rights movement practice: Organizations with printing budgets like the NAACP and CORE routinely created signs for protests, but participants could make and bring their own if they wished. Many local actions didn't even include signs; the presence of bodies—especially Black bodies—where they were not supposed to be, whether that was sitting at a lunch counter or blocking a street, was signifier enough. Where civil rights demonstrators did carry posters at local protests, they were generally handmade; the invention of the Magic Marker in the mid-1950s had made sign making a quick, easy, and affordable matter. Images from the big Detroit Walk to Freedom earlier that summer show a vibrant mix of official and homemade placards, with plenty of the latter. If fear of unruliness and disorder was the backdrop for the decision to control the signs at the 1963 March on Washington, an expansive and rather commanding vision of leadership was required to implement it.[10]

As the planning proceeded, there was pushback from local organizers about this limitation; some groups quite understandably wanted to carry their own signs and devise their own slogans. After some debate, the leadership had to loosen up a little on their control over the placards. The National Committee still directed which slogans would be allowed—staff members and interested collaborators like famed labor leader Moe Foner drafted long lists for them to consider—but some groups were allowed to make and bring their own signs so long as they limited themselves to the authorized messages. Certain categories of preapproved organizations— religious groups, labor unions, fraternal organizations, and of course the

The Detroit Walk to Freedom, the first mass protest march in American history, held two months before the 1963 March on Washington.

sponsoring civil rights groups—were also allowed to bring "signs of identification," advertising their participation in the event. But, they were admonished, "such identification should carry only the name of the organization; no slogans are permitted." And no one else was supposed to carry any poster or placard that was not provided by organizers. This policy was emphatically not a mere request. The marshals for the march—a force of some two thousand off-duty Black police officers, firefighters, and prison guards—were tasked, among other things, with "policing picket signs," as the NAACP's full-time staff person for the march, John Morsell, phrased it. Anyone carrying an unauthorized sign was to be handled under the

Volunteers prepare thousands of signs for the 1963 March on Washington.

standard protocol for disrupters: "Detect, point out, and encircle offenders, using at all times nonviolent persuasion to control the situation."[11]

Black nationalist leader Malcolm X, whose political differences with the march organizers were far-reaching, characterized the handling of the signs as one of numerous reasons why he decided to boycott the march. Plenty of people in direct-action-oriented groups like SNCC and CORE were angered by the decision to scrap the initial plans for civil disobedience and only reluctantly went along with a plan of action they found tame. Malcolm X went much further, emphatically refusing to participate in an event that allowed so little political autonomy. "There wasn't a single logistics aspect uncontrolled," he explained in his 1964 autobiography. "The marchers had been instructed to bring no signs—signs were provided. . . . They had been told *how* to arrive, *when, where* to arrive, *where* to assemble, when to *start* marching, the *route* to march."[12]

He had a point. The sea of uniform signs at the March on Washington reflected a certain key quality to the march organizing: a directive leadership style that in many respects stood at odds, quite deliberately, with the impatient and restive grassroots. You didn't have to belong to the Nation of Islam to find this level of control off-putting. It was out of step with the broad direction not just of the grassroots civil rights movement, but of many parts of the left, especially the nascent New Left. New ideas were in the air about what leadership should look like and how groups should be structured, and the movements with the most new energy and momentum, from SNCC to Students for a Democratic Society (SDS), which had been founded the previous year, were experimenting with organizing methods, group structures, and forms of decision making that were decentralized, inclusive, and participatory.

The differences in organizing styles can't be reduced to any single factor, but some were matters of political and ideological habit. Attempts by segregationists like Alabama governor George Wallace to paint the main march organizers as Communists failed miserably, because they simply weren't true. It was well known that Rustin had once been a Communist Party member, but he had left because of political differences way back in 1941; none of the other key organizers were members, and indeed quite a few were vehemently anti-Communist. Many key march planners were, however, socialists, and a number of them belonged to a small party-style group of the anti-Communist left, the Young People's Socialist League (YPSL), that featured a centralized organizational structure, top-down leadership, and a penchant for asserting political control through backroom machinations. March staffers Rachelle Horowitz and Tom Kahn were key leaders of YPSL, which had tried, and failed, to take over SDS early on in order to steer its politics in a more traditionally Old Left direction. Others who were centrally involved in the march organizing, such as administrative committee chair Cleveland Robinson, came from parts of the labor movement where hierarchical structures and centralized decision making were standard and unquestioned organizational traits. If there was a whiff of Leninism in the repeated emphasis on "discipline" and "order" in the planning meetings and organizational materials, it surely flowed from these Old Left affiliations. Rigid control of political behavior—and messaging—was a long-standing practice in these precincts of the left.[13]

Gender also played a notable part. Within the grassroots civil rights movement, Black women like Ella Baker of SNCC and Septima Clark of the SCLC were at the forefront of pioneering empowering new approaches in their organizing work, but neither they nor any other women had a voice

Organizers A. Philip Randolph, Roy Wilkins of the NAACP, and Anna Arnold Hedgeman of the National Council of Churches, the only woman with any official role in the 1963 march planning.

Septima Clark (second from left) meets with a group of students at the Highlander Folk School in Tennessee, 1958.

in the top march leadership. Indeed, women weren't just sidelined from any decision making or other prominent role in the March on Washington; the decisions to exclude them were made in the most peremptory way possible, as if the matter hardly warranted serious consideration. Early in the march planning, Anna Arnold Hedgeman, a longtime civil rights organizer who was part of the National Council of Churches' Commission on Religion and Race and the only woman on either of the march leadership bodies (she was appointed to the larger, less powerful administrative committee), urged Randolph to expand that committee to involve key Black women's organizations, including the National Association of Colored Women's Clubs and the National Council of Negro Women. These organizations had vast reach. In 1963, the NCNW alone had a larger membership than that of the NAACP, which had been allowed to veto plans for civil disobedience because its organizational resources and half-million members were viewed as crucial to the march's success. The women who made up the active base of these clubs and local organizations had long played highly consequential grassroots roles in the civil rights movement. Hedgeman hadn't even requested that these groups be included in the powerful National Committee, though it makes for an interesting thought experiment to imagine what might have happened if they had been; she was requesting only that they have a central and recognized role in implementing those leaders' decisions. "As usual, the men must have discussed the matter in my absence," she later recalled. The proposal was rejected out of hand, without even informing her.[14]

The divergent organizing visions were captured in a story recounted by Septima Clark, whose citizenship schools in the Deep South were providing an important model for grassroots empowerment. "I sent a letter to Dr. King asking him not to lead all the marches himself but instead to develop leaders who could lead their own marches," she explained. "Dr. King read that letter before the staff. It just tickled them; they just laughed." Attempts to have a woman included among the march speakers were no more successful than Hedgeman's effort to bring more women into the administrative committee. Appeals to the leadership continued right up to the morning of the march, to no effect. John Morsell, the NAACP representative on the administrative committee, described the effort in terms that reflect how disdainfully the leadership viewed these appeals:

"We became aware that there was some resentment on the distaff side, because it was all men and Anna Hedgeman who is a great feminist was all swollen up because there was no woman." It was a total shutout. Recalled Dorothy Height, president of the National Council of Negro Women at the time, "Nothing that the women said or did broke the impasse blocking their participation. I've never seen a more immovable force."[15]

If a certain directive masculinity shaped the march organizing, it's important to underscore that it was a Black masculinity, and that gave it a different significance both within the movement and within American society at large. A. Philip Randolph had long embraced a vision of civil rights centered on the notion of "manhood rights," uplifting the status and dignity of Black men as a central part of the struggle for racial justice; the distinct problems facing Black women went mostly unmentioned. Rustin, King, and many other civil rights leaders shared elements of that view, and it shaped the movement's overall discourse and demands. The second most famous set of printed protest signs in American history, after the ones at the March on Washington, may be the "I AM A MAN" signs carried by striking sanitation workers in Memphis in 1968—the simple fact of asserting Black men's humanity and masculinity was a profound challenge to the existing racial order. That made sexism within the civil rights movement a more delicate and complex matter than the sexism of, say, the white left during this period. For the time being, Black women in the movement mostly kept their frustrations with male leadership out of public view. They knew what the men would not acknowledge through formal power sharing: The movement's backbone was women. As Coretta Scott King put it in 1966, "Women have been the ones who have made it possible for the movement to be a mass movement."[16]

Administrative and clerical staff at the March on Washington office in Harlem, summer 1963. Photo by Werner Wolff

Women were sidelined from any official role in the march or its leadership, but the evidence suggests that they carried out a great deal of the actual work of getting huge numbers of people to come to DC. It took an enormous amount of coordination to reach out to potential supporters on a mass scale, persuade them to join the march, and get them safely to and from the event. Some of the mobilizing took place through exhortation, as King and other leaders took to the media, or to their pulpits, to encourage participation. High-profile entertainers like Harry Belafonte and Sidney Poitier also helped spread the word. But a great deal of the outreach came through much more direct, face-to-face means, like street leafleting, and through formal and informal networks like clubs and social groups; national protests rely on local organizing. Black women had long been instrumental in anchoring this kind of grassroots work within the civil rights movement—to an important extent, mobilizing was informally defined as women's work, going back at least to Montgomery in 1955, when women launched the famous bus boycott by secretly hand-distributing some fifty thousand leaflets to nearly every Black home in the city within twenty-four hours of Rosa Parks's arrest. (Male leaders, including Dr. King, stepped in and took over formal leadership of the boycott the next day, without even including the women in the meeting where they assumed control.) In much of the civil rights movement, as in many other movements to come, "Men led, but women organized," to quote historian Charles Payne's pithy summary. Women's energies and expertise were instrumental in spurring large numbers to attend the March on Washington, even as women were denied any official recognition or decision-making power.[17]

Rustin's long experience as a protest organizer gave him a deep understanding of how delicate it could be to try to steer a movement as completely as the march leadership was seeking to do, and in one staff meeting he even joked about the imperiousness of the decision-making process. Rachelle Horowitz, the march's transportation coordinator, recalled a "hilarious" staff discussion of how the leaders wanted to handle everything from the signs to the food that marchers should bring. "The staff at that point was all involved with all the more intricate questions that were then going to be presented to the administrative committee and the Big Ten—they included where we were going to march—how much they will speak," Horowitz recalled in 1967. "At one point during the discussion the question of lunch [came] up and Bayard announces they are going to put in the manual that people should bring peanut butter and jelly sandwiches, and I looked up and innocently said, 'Peanut butter and jelly?' and he said, 'Don't argue about this, when the Big Ten have decided.'"[18]

It was no joke, though: The lines of authority were clear. The Big Ten were to lead—and the marchers were to follow. They were to speak—and the crowd was to listen. Few remember this fact, but all ten men delivered speeches that day, with King's legendary address coming so late in a long day that the crowd was weary and many marchers had already begun to depart. Though funds for the march were tight, Rustin had made a special point of ordering a very expensive top-of-the-line sound system to ensure the crowd remained an audience. "Once you get that many people they are, essentially no matter what other factors are involved, a mob, unless they can hear," Rustin explained in an interview four years after the event, an assertion that would of course be disproved at dozens of mass protests to come. Passivity was built into the March on Washington planning: Participants were mobilized as bodies, but not as voices. This quality even extended to the way the musical entertainment was handled. In a striking departure from the usual movement practice of joining together in singing freedom songs as a crucial expression of collective engagement and solidarity, none of the performers at the Lincoln Memorial invited the crowd to join in.[19]

Not everyone who attended the huge and historic event was willing to give up their autonomy so readily. Plenty of people, of course, sang without invitation, at many points throughout the day. A small number of marchers defied the leadership's instructions and brought their own signs—most notably, representatives of some of the intense local struggles that had unfolded earlier in the summer and others who wished to bear witness to the incredible violence and suffering that local movements had experienced. A group from Americus, Georgia, where dozens had been beaten and arrested at protests outside a segregated movie theater in July, carried a sign that detailed some of the injuries they had sustained: "Milton Wilkerson—20 stitches. Emanuel McClendon—3 stitches (Age 67). James Williams—broken leg." Eighteen-year-old James Lee Pruitt, who had been jailed for fifty-two days earlier that summer for taking part in a local voting rights protest in Greenwood, Mississippi, also brought a handmade sign. Its message could hardly be characterized as inflammatory: "We Must Have the Vote in Mississippi by 1964," it read. But Pruitt's slogan, however heartfelt and noncontroversial, was not included among the authorized ones, so marshals for the march followed protocol, surrounding him and taking him into a tent for questioning. Only after they had detained him for a time was he able to persuade them to let him keep his sign and participate in the march.[20]

Dr. King's resounding speech is of course the most famous element of the March on Washington. Accounts of the day typically feature images from the rally, where King spoke and the audience listened, and not the march, the part of the day's program where the crowd participated most actively. But there is one oft-recounted moment from the march, and it reveals much about the event's underlying character. The march was only supposed to step off once the ten leaders were arrayed in a big line at the front for the news cameras. (Coretta Scott King and other wives of the leaders were not allowed to march with them; they marched separately, over on Independence Avenue.) The crowd was restless, though, and in no mood to wait,

Joining in song at the 1963 March on Washington.
Photo by Leonard Freed

MARTYR MEDGAR EVERS

THE BLACK MAN FELL AND HELPLESS LAY,
A GAPING WOUND UPON HIS BACK,
A WITNESS TO THE SAVAGE WAY
A BEAST HAD MADE HIS FOUL ATTACK.

HIS WOUND PUKED OUT HIS NOBLE BLOOD,
HIS BLOOD SANK DEEP IN FREEDOM'S SOIL.
"MY GOD!" HIS WIFE CRIED OUT. "MY GOD!"
IS T-H-I-S REWARD FOR FREEDOM'S TOIL?

"WHERE IS THE JUSTICE IN THIS LAND,
THAT LOUDLY TOLLS THE FREEDOM BELL,
WHILE TYRANTS RULE WITH A FREE HAND
COMMITTING ALL THE SINS OF HELL?"

OLE GLORY'S TARNISHED WITH HIS BLOOD,
FOR HAVING SHABBILY ALLOWED
A NOBLE SON TO BE DOWNTROD

University
of California
Alumni

WE
MARCH
JOBS
NOW

Three young women at the 1963 March on Washington in front of an
unauthorized sign memorializing slain NAACP leader Medgar Evers. Photo by
Marion K. Trikosko

and people began marching before the men had lined up to lead them. The marshals had to scramble to open up sufficient space in the moving mass of bodies for the leaders to take their places, and to hold the line long enough for photographers to memorialize the moment. "There was all kinds of frantic dashing around, getting the cards up front, trying to stop the movement of the crowd," remembered John Morsell of the NAACP. The Big Ten amused each other by recounting the old line, "There go the people. I must follow them, for I am their leader." Recalled Morsell, "If that joke was told once that afternoon, it was told a million times. Everybody felt it was the only appropriate thing to say."[21]

There were, in fact, plenty of other things one could say about that moment. You might even call it a synecdoche for the March on Washington's relationship to the larger movement of the time. The march leadership had, in every sense, inserted themselves in a popular groundswell in order to steer it, and they could only do that by slowing it down and holding it back. The march was as much about constraining the unruly energies of the grassroots as it was about applying pressure on the Kennedy administration, channeling vast anger and frustration into something as neat and bounded as a preprinted picket sign, in the hope that doing so would make the appeal for change impossible to ignore or reject. In a 1964 essay, SNCC organizer Michael Thelwell reflected on the march: "On the one hand, there was an undeniable grandeur and awesomeness about the mighty river of humanity, more people than most of us will ever see again in one place, affirming in concert their faith in an idea, and in a hope that is just." But, he continued, "It is sad that at the end of so much activity, the best and worst that could be said is that 'it was orderly and no one was offended.'"[22]

Lining up the leaders in the midst of the march. Roy Wilkins of the NAACP and A. Philip Randolph are at the far right.

The march in progress. Photo by Warren K. Leffler

Though the 1963 March on Washington is widely treated as the epit-ome of the big protest march in America, there never would be another one quite like it. No other protest would serve as a movement touchstone in quite the same way that that march has done for the Black freedom strug-gle. No other protest would be sanctified and mythologized to the same degree, either; every sizable subsequent mobilization would be compared to the 1963 March on Washington and somehow found to fall short. There would never be another demonstration in America that people would so emphatically credit with achieving a major legislative goal, even though the claim is a stretch at best, and no subsequent protest would be shaped and tamed so extensively by a sitting president and his administration. No one would ever try to stage manage a large crowd of demonstrators so tightly again, and no large crowd would again cooperate so willingly with

The Fifth Avenue Peace Parade, one of the earliest sizable protests against the Vietnam War. The photo likely dates from the first event in October 1965.

being cast in such a scripted role. The flawless execution of the event on that August day in 1963 meant that future organizers would not have to contend with quite the same barriers of fear. The March on Washington for Jobs and Freedom opened up both literal and metaphorical space for political action, in ways that constitute one of its most enduring contributions. If that initially came only through highly respectable and stage-managed means, it set a precedent for mass protest, and mass assembly, that future movements would build on. By the 2017 Women's Marches, the hallmark of a successful mass mobilization would typically be the diversity rather than the homogeneity of the voices and messages on display.

Certainly no one would ever again imagine they could completely control the signs at a major protest. There was a noteworthy attempt to

Demonstrators outside the White House at a November 1965 antiwar protest in Washington, DC. Photo by Theodore B. Hetzel

do so at one of the earliest large protests against the Vietnam War, the October 1965 Fifth Avenue Peace Parade in New York. Organizers were so split over whether to call for an immediate military withdrawal from Vietnam or for negotiations to end the conflict that they ended up authorizing just one slogan for the event, a lowest-common-denominator message that all could support: "Stop the War Now." Though the signs all said the same thing, in practice the march was far more freewheeling than the 1963 March on Washington. The culture of self-expression that would shape the New Left and its activist practice was already in evidence. Many participants didn't just carry (approved) signs, but also expressed their political views through the political buttons they wore. Some wore skeleton masks and played musical instruments, and others carried evocative protest props like a blood-soaked Uncle Sam, pointing the way toward rich traditions of protest art that would develop in the years and decades to come. By November 1965, when the National Committee for a Sane Nuclear Policy (SANE) organized the first major antiwar march in Washington, DC, the notion of controlling protest signs had been largely abandoned. SANE hoped to keep the messages of "kooks, communists or draft-dodgers" out of their march and compiled a list of seventeen acceptable slogans for the day. But they knew enough to bow to the evolving political realities of mass mobilizations. While SANE did have about two hundred march monitors on hand to request the removal of unauthorized signs or messages (a tenth the number of marshals at the March on Washington), they decided they would take no stronger action if people refused to comply. "We'll just ignore them," said march coordinator Sanford Gottlieb of unapproved slogans, "and they will just get lost in the crowd."[23]

No big protest in America will ever look like the 1963 March on Washington again, with all the signs controlled by a central leadership. But you often see a sea of similar signs at large protests, and when you do, you're usually seeing an organization flexing its muscles. (Advances in printing technology have also made it viable for individuals or small groups to shoulder the cost of large-format printing since at least the late 1980s, when the AIDS activist group ACT UP upended long-standing practices of protest signage with its bold and media-savvy designs; when you see uniformly printed signs at smaller protests, especially at direct actions, you're often seeing groups that have consciously carried forward this newer tradition of art-directed activism.) When organizations have signs printed up for a big demonstration, they're typically seeking to signal not just their message, but their organizational might and presence. Perhaps the signs were made by the sponsoring entity, whether a single organization or a coalition of multiple groups, and are publicizing the agreed-upon theme or demands of the event; perhaps they were made by coalition partners or cosponsoring groups and are showcasing their participation as well as their political stance.[24]

Colorful printed signs predominated, for instance, at one of the very largest protest marches ever to take place in Washington, DC, the enormous March for Women's Lives in April 2004, a collaboration between the National Organization for Women (NOW), the National Abortion Rights Action League (NARAL), Planned Parenthood, and other established organizations. Turnout figures for this event are disputed, as they are for most big protests, but organizers could credibly claim that more than a million marched that day in support of women's reproductive rights. The mobilization followed on the heels of a series of large pro-choice protests that NOW had organized in 1986, 1989, and 1992 in response to mounting threats to reproductive rights, leveraging its organizational resources time and again to bring impressive crowds to the streets of DC. Signs printed by NOW and its allies were foregrounded at each of these events. Instead of prohibiting messages they don't like, organizations typically flood the crowd, and especially the highly visible lead contingent, with signs they've produced. (Nobody left a march step-off to chance again after 1963; organizers typically take special care to be sure they line up the front of their marches, usually with a special lead banner, before anyone starts moving.)

It's tricky, though, to assess a group's real contributions from the signs featured at a protest. All you can tell for certain is that the group had a

The 2004 March for Women's Lives, one of the largest demonstrations ever held in the United States, gets ready to step off. Photo by Susan Walsh

printing budget and enough staff or volunteer capacity to distribute posters. Signs can deceive. There are certain quite small but fervent organizations that reliably show up with big piles of posters at mass protests; the signs offer a way for them to promote their political analysis and, even more, to create the illusion of broader political support than they actually enjoy. More generally, unless you speak to the people who are carrying preprinted signs at a protest, you can never be sure whether they are active members of an organization who are proudly displaying their affiliation or just individuals who happen to be carrying signs that someone was handing out that day. Signs can advertise the presence of an organized contingent—say, members of a labor union or a faith-based group who came to a protest together and are showcasing their collective might—or they can give the impression of a greater degree of connection than actually exists. With each decade that has passed since the original March on Washington, there are fewer and fewer large organizations with a close and strong enough relationship to their base that they can directly mobilize their members. These sorts of locally rooted voluntary associations with robust member participation have been in steady decline since the 1960s, largely through slow attrition, though in some key cases (as with the labor movement in general, and the community organizing group ACORN) as a result of concerted right-wing attacks. They've been supplanted by what scholar Theda Skocpol describes as "professionally managed advocacy groups without chapters or members," which have a top-heavy structure and whose work is driven by paid staff. This shift to what other critics have termed a "nonprofit industrial complex" has accelerated with the rise of digital organizing; these types of organizations typically have subscribers, followers, and donors, but few ways for supporters to participate more actively. A uniformity of signs at any protest brings a great clarity of message, but it can be difficult to discern how robust and resilient the underlying movement is, or if there's a movement—instead of, say, an email list—represented there at all.[25]

The kind of popular power on display when organizations lead their memberships into action, as NOW did with its marches in the 1980s and early 1990s, may be muscular, but it is increasingly rare; few sizable organizations have memberships that are mobilizable in quite that way. Big mobilizations typically involve a more fragile and less predictable kind of

A marcher holds up one of hundreds of signs provided by the Human Rights Campaign Fund at the 1993 March on Washington for Lesbian, Gay and Bi Equal Rights and Liberation. Photo by Howard Sachs

popular power, and their success generally depends on the participation of large numbers of people who aren't affiliated with any group. Even the 1963 March on Washington, typically thought of as the product of its sponsoring organizations, owed its then-unprecedented size to mobilizing the unorganized. Their participation likely accounted for at least half of the crowd who gathered in DC. On the eve of the march, transportation coordinator Rachelle Horowitz tallied up all the people planning to come to the event through official channels, and the number who had reserved seats on buses, trains, and planes through participating groups totaled 110,000. The extra margin of more or less spontaneous participation by some

140,000 other people—tens of thousands of DC locals, plus people who had arranged their own last-minute transportation—made the crucial difference between a solidly successful event and a gathering that was and felt truly massive. Even Horowitz's tally gives a somewhat distorted impression of how the mobilizing worked. Although organizations like churches, civic groups, and NAACP chapters were responsible for lining up the transportation, a high proportion of their tickets were sold to unaffiliated individuals who had been moved to participate by news reports or other face-to-face outreach efforts like volunteer street leafleting. "People all kind of started calling up at the office," Horowitz recalled. "In fact the March itself was not sending any buses, because we couldn't you know worry about any bus captains collecting the money from individual fares. But people would be calling all the time, and I would continually have to tell New York CORE that they had to take another bus." New York CORE and many other groups that arranged bus transportation sold a significant portion of the seats to people who weren't official members but wanted a way to take part in the historic march.[26]

A crucial challenge for organizers in the wake of any big mobilization is how to absorb the new political energy and the new movement participants into some ongoing effort. Ideally, people should go home from a major demonstration not only with a feeling that they have played a role in something larger than themselves, but with a commitment to continued action and a clear sense of how they might contribute. For all the many ways in which the 1963 March on Washington can be considered an unqualified success, it's worth noting that from the narrow perspective of movement building, its impact was at best muted, both for the organizations behind it and for the grassroots civil rights movement more generally.

March organizers had a plan for bringing the waves of unaffiliated people who came to DC into movement organizations afterward: They distributed pledge cards, about 75,000 of which they collected from the crowd. Each of the six sponsoring organizations were given copies of these cards, in the hope that they would use them to expand their membership. Evidence suggests that the NAACP may have been the only group that managed to follow up, and they did so mostly by sending fund appeals. The NAACP's membership ranks surged, but only briefly, and there's little evidence that the march brought in many new active participants in the group's local chapters. Many local groups were exhausted by the work involved in building participation for the march; the effort of mobilizing, ironically enough, seemed to demobilize ongoing grassroots work.[27]

This sense of depletion was felt most strongly in the more direct-action-oriented parts of the movement, where enthusiasm for the march had been tempered with reservations from the start. Michael Thelwell of SNCC wrote in 1964, "The March became a symbol and a focal point in the minds of Negroes during this explosive summer of our discontent, and in many communities where the Negro temper was right, and where there had begun meaningful protest activity, the militants were diverted into mobilization for the March. . . . This happened in too many areas; local action slowed down, and we all looked to Washington for the climax that never came." James Farmer, the national chairman of CORE, offered an even more pessimistic assessment in a 1967 interview: "I think we would have to say that the March sounded the death bell of the activist movement. Our chapters began to decline after the March and action began to decline. Many people who had been active said well we've done it, we really did it." In his bitterness from the vantage point of four years later, when many felt

Police work to remove a protester locked to a construction crane in an action against hiring discrimination in the building trades, Queens, New York, September 1963.

the movement had reached an impasse, Farmer no doubt overstated the case. Some people went back home after the grand march and felt they'd done their part, but actions by CORE and other groups certainly continued. By fall, though, you could already sense a turn to stronger methods and angrier rhetoric in some movement circles, evidence of the climate of frustration and harbingers of the coming rise of Black Power. About a week after the march, for instance, protesters in Queens continued an

Protesters block a police cruiser containing fellow demonstrators who were arrested during an action against hiring discrimination at a local bank, St. Louis, October 1963. Photo by Robert Larouche

ongoing campaign against discrimination in the building trades by breaking into a construction site and locking themselves to a crane. That's the sort of tactic you use when milder methods like pickets—or mass marches— don't seem to be working. (The judge who handled their case gravely declared, in what might be the first recorded instance of the march being used to chastise subsequent protesters, "The demonstrators in Washington were wonderful. You people are accused of flaunting the law daily in your demonstration.") That October, young protesters who had been trying without success to pressure a St. Louis bank to hire more Black employees escalated their campaign by lying down in front of a police cruiser that was taking their fellow demonstrators to jail. The march had elevated and celebrated King's dream of racial justice in ways that would inspire people for decades, but that didn't mean its effects could be felt in the near term among those working at the grassroots to make the dream a concrete reality—a point worth bearing in mind when reading the snap assessments that follow any given protest.[28]

The morning after the March on Washington, before the experience had hardened into myth, the *New York Times* described the event as "a day of sad music, strange silences and good feeling in the streets." At the conclusion of the march, A. Philip Randolph read out the text of the pledge, in which marchers promised that they would "not relax until victory is won." Then, for the first and only time at the carefully orchestrated event, the crowd was invited to speak. They were given three words to say, "I so pledge." And then they went home, with posters in hand as souvenirs of a historic day that had pioneered mass protest in America, in majestic but massively controlled form. A US Information Agency film captured the carefully staged drama of the day, and turned it into overseas propaganda touting the strength of American democracy, even as the Kennedy administration continued to drag its heels on meaningful racial reform.[29]

> **The aftermath of the 1963 March on Washington.**
> Photo by Leonard Freed

Fast forward to January 21, 2017, the day after Donald Trump's inauguration, when an astonishing 4.2 million or more people took to the streets in more than 650 coordinated Women's Marches all around the United States. A great many large protests had happened in the interim, but this day of action was larger than any of them. Everything about the Women's Marches, from the number of events to the overall turnout, broke or rivaled records for prior outpourings of popular dissent in America, making it almost certainly the largest coordinated protest ever in US history. The day's hundreds of demonstrations were anchored by a major march in Washington, DC, that flooded the nation's capital with 800,000 or more protesters. As such,

The 2017 Women's March fills Forty-Second Street in New York. Photo by Carolina Kroon the Washington component of the day ranked as one of the district's largest protest gatherings, with a turnout at least three times greater than that of the 1963 march. Only three previous Washington protests—the 1993 Lesbian, Gay and Bi March on Washington, the 1995 Million Man March, and the 2004 March for Women's Lives—rivaled it in size. The DC event was so immense that organizers never quite corralled it into a single, unitary march; crowds flowed like water through the streets and open spaces of the city. All around the country, turnout for the local "sister marches" ranged from solid to stunning: A crowd of 100,000 marched in Denver, and some 650,000 filled the streets of Los Angeles. In Chicago, the crowd of at least a quarter million was so large that city officials said it would be unsafe for them to march, but people marched anyway, peacefully overwhelming the Loop and many city streets. In New York, people were packed so tightly that they could barely make their way across town, and the march stalled repeatedly from human gridlock. In many smaller locales, turnout was the highest for any demonstration ever staged there. At least 10,000 people assembled in Reno, Helena, and Lansing; around 15,000 marched in St. Louis and Nashville; while in St. Petersburg, Florida, the crowd topped 20,000. Many small towns witnessed impressive turnouts for their size: 320 in Kodiak, Alaska, a town of just over 6,000; and 700 in Sharon, Pennsylvania, whose population is roughly 13,000.[30]

Their scale, though, was only one quality that set the Women's Marches apart from previous big mobilizations in US history. The most obvious difference, of course, was that these were *Women's* Marches. Washington had certainly witnessed feminist mobilizations before, including a march for the Equal Rights Amendment in 1978 and the series of major reproductive rights demonstrations that culminated with the enormous March

The 2017 Women's March in Kodiak, Alaska. Photo by Judy Heller

for Women's Lives in 2004. But these events were all far more narrowly focused than the huge outpouring in 2017. The Women's Marches were led and shaped by women, but with a sweeping and inclusive agenda of issues that cut across demographic lines. That composition and breadth of focus would carry over to every aspect of the resistance to Trump, a sprawling movement of movements that has been overwhelmingly composed of women. As they marched, women were, in essence, laying claim to leadership of the left, staking out political space for a broad grassroots

Sea of signs at the 2017 Women's March in Madison, Wisconsin.   Photo by Paul McMahon

progressivism with feminism—and the much-maligned identity politics—at its core. In the year after Trump took office, women constituted a majority at protest after protest. When it came to grassroots organizing, the gender gap was even greater. The thousands of local resistance groups that sprang up to oppose Trump and Trumpism were typically started by women, and women often constituted 70 or 80 percent of their active membership. Women made some 86 percent of protest phone calls to Congress in the months after the new president took office and also took the lead in using stronger resistance tactics, from blockading Trump Tower in support of immigrant rights to holding sit-ins at Senate offices to defend access to health care.[31]

If you glanced at any one of the 2017 Women's Marches, you could read this women-led, multi-issue character in the powerful signs that people displayed. In a striking contrast to the 1963 March on Washington and most past major protests, those who took to the streets in such impressive numbers in 2017 mostly carried signs that they had carefully and thoughtfully made themselves. Instead of one single slogan or set of approved messages, there was an exuberant array of sentiments, giving a rich sense of the priorities of the crowds: "Women Rise Up," "My Body My Choice," "White Silence = Violence," "Trans Lives Matter," "Democracy for All," "Feminism Must Be Intersectional," "Hear Our Voice," "None of This Is Normal," and thousands upon thousands more. People made posters celebrating values and principles: democracy, diversity, equality, justice. They displayed messages of love and peace and connection, alongside angry insults aimed at the new president and his enablers.

Environmentalism, immigrant rights, racial justice, climate justice, and lesbian, gay, and transgender rights were all featured, signaling the presence of movements that had arisen or persisted during the Obama years, such as Black Lives Matter and the nationwide anti-pipeline movement sparked by Native American resistance at Standing Rock. Plenty of people made their hand-lettered march signs at home alone before the event, but many gathered for poster-making parties that prefigured the decentralized, locally based organizing that would characterize the resistance going forward. People gathered to make signs at churches in Anchorage, Alaska, and Grand Rapids, Michigan, and at public libraries in Tucson, Arizona, and New Haven, Connecticut. They decorated posters at a yoga studio in Helena, Montana, and at a pop-up bookstore in Miami, Florida. The signs were so creative and so full of heart and passion that taking in their messages and spirit became one of the most memorable aspects of the day. Slideshows of signs were everywhere on the internet, and two quick photo compilations were published soon after (both benefiting feminist and progressive nonprofits) to "serve as beacons of vigilance and hope," in the words of Najeebah Al-Ghadban, the designer of one of the books. Numerous museums, including the National Museum of American History and the Worcester Art Museum in Massachusetts, collected signs from the marches to preserve as part of their collections.[32]

Above and beyond the many slogans they featured, the signs' handmade character sent its own signal, reflecting a do-it-yourself quality that shaped the entire mobilization, from the way the marches first popped up on Facebook to the crowdsourcing apps that people used to make bus reservations, bypassing a key role—renting and filling buses—that organizations had traditionally played in protests. Of course there were preprinted posters sprinkled through the crowds, just as there were buses chartered by groups in the traditional way. The National Organization for Women,

The 2017 Women's March in Los Angeles. Photo by Brendan Buckley

Planned Parenthood, the American Civil Liberties Union, and numerous other established organizations threw their weight behind the march organizing, and advertised their involvement by handing out signs at some of the marches. A number of labor unions, including the Service Employees International Union and UNITE HERE, mobilized contingents that featured their signs. The Women's March national team held a design competition and had official posters printed up featuring the winning entries, and artist Shepard Fairey adapted his famous 2008 Barack Obama "Hope" poster into three designs for the occasion. But in city after city, so many people decided to make their own signs for the Women's Marches that retailers

Trio of protesters at the 2017 Women's March in St. Louis. Photo by Carrie Zukoski

had trouble keeping art supplies in stock that month. Sales of foam-core boards soared by 42 percent over the previous year, and sales of paint markers jumped by 35 percent. In just the week before people marched around the country, some 2 million poster boards were sold nationwide.[33]

The profusion of colorful handmade signs was a powerful clue to another quality that made the Women's Marches distinctive: the viral, decentralized way the events were organized. The marches came together through a process that was unlike any other prior protest mobilization in America, and the differences profoundly shaped the character of the anti-Trump resistance that followed in their wake. The idea to hold the country's first national mass protest, the 1963 March on Washington, sprang from the political imagination of seasoned civil rights organizers with decades of experience under their belts. The Women's Marches, by contrast, famously began with a couple of Facebook posts by two women who had never planned a protest before. The march's origin story has now been told many times: The event was first proposed in an election night post by Teresa Shook, a retired attorney in Hawaii, in Pantsuit Nation, a private pro-Hillary Facebook group whose membership had soared in the period just before and after Election Day. By the time Shook woke up the next morning, some 10,000 people had already responded to her event invitation. A similar and nearly simultaneous Facebook post by New York fashion designer Bob Bland also went immediately viral. "In the span of 48 hours, the page says there's 75,000 people interested. And then it was 150,000 people. And soon 250,000 people," said Bland, recalling the extraordinary speed with which the event spread online. "It was very much like a spontaneous groundswell that started the night of November 8," remembered Mrinalini Chakraborty, who jumped into the organizing that next morning, ultimately becoming the national field director for the Women's March. "It was almost like a nation had awoken."[34]

No sooner had the idea begun to take off, though, than problems arose. Shook had initially called her event the "Million Woman March," unaware both of the huge Black-led 1997 Philadelphia event that first bore that name—a major gathering of Black women with hundreds of thousands of people in attendance—and of how controversial it would be for a white organizer to appropriate it. The social media criticism was swift and massive, calling out the racial blinders that had led to the choice of name and the need for multiracial leadership, especially given that 53 percent of white women voters had just backed an openly racist presidential candidate. "We realized we hadn't really thought about who was going to lead this," Bland later noted. "We were just organizing as a bunch of people, and it was just like this huge, viral thing. And at that point, people said, 'Look, y'all are white. Like all of y'all.' And we were like, 'Oh, shit. Yeah, you're right.'"[35]

After a flurry of behind-the-scenes meetings and phone calls, three experienced women of color organizers—Carmen Perez, Tamika Mallory, and Linda Sarsour—quickly stepped up to serve along with Bland as national co-chairs of the march and to assemble an organizing team. "For the first time in history on a mass scale, this was going to be a major movement for everyone, that was being led by women of color, and women of color were fighting at the table as leaders," recalled Paola Mendoza, another early team member, who served as the march's artistic director. The naming of the co-chairs created both direct and symbolic links with the organizing of the 1963 March on Washington. Both Perez and Mallory had been mentored by Harry Belafonte, the eminent performer and civil rights activist who had played a variety of roles in the 1963 march organizing: Perez had served as executive director of Belafonte's nonprofit, The Gathering for Justice, since 2010, and Mallory, the past executive director of Al Sharpton's National Action Network, was a lead organizer of the 50th Anniversary March on Washington in 2013, at which tens of thousands commemorated the historic event. With the new team agreeing on the necessity of a name change for the 2017 protests, Mallory drew on her long-standing connections to contact Dr. King's daughter, Bernice King, and with her blessing, the team officially renamed the DC event the

Women's March on Washington, very consciously choosing to echo the name of the protest that first filled the streets of the nation's capital with calls for justice. Fifty-four years after Black women had been both literally and figuratively sidelined from any leadership role in the 1963 march, women of color took the helm in organizing the Women's March on Washington, giving the 2017 event an intersectional feminist framing that had never before been front and center at any major protest in America.[36]

The co-chairs and their team of collaborators had almost exactly the same frenetically short lead time to pull the event together that organizers had had in 1963, and their work had a similar improvised quality, but the reasons were quite different. Holding a mass protest march was of course no longer a novel thing to do—the tactic had become ritualized over the intervening half century. But the process of making it happen was quite different in 2017. In the very broadest sense, no one—and certainly no organization—set the mobilizing in motion for the 2017 Women's Marches. People at the grassroots level spontaneously mobilized themselves, and organizers everywhere were constantly scrambling to keep up.

To say this is not to minimize the extraordinary amount of organizing work that still needed to happen to make the events safe and successful. As Chakraborty put it, "It's almost amusing to me when I hear people saying things like, 'Oh, people would have showed up anyway.' Mobilizations don't just happen—there are people pulling a million strings to make sure that it happens without chaos and that it happens well." There were permits to negotiate, bus parking to arrange, portable toilets to rent, speakers and sound equipment to line up, volunteers to recruit and train, and many more logistical details to manage. In 2017, much of this work was coordinated online or through conference calls in a way that simply hadn't been

Organizers of the 2017 Women's March on Washington in a final planning meeting. Co-chair Tamika Mallory is at left, and co-chairs Carmen Perez and Linda Sarsour are at right. Photo by Kisha Bari

possible in 1963. The organizing wasn't spearheaded by any single group or in any single office, and much of the national organizing team didn't meet face-to-face until just days before the march.[37]

They led, but the kind of leadership they provided was quite different in style and conception from the leadership provided by men like Randolph, Rustin, and King a half century before. If anything, it carried forward the organizing traditions that those at the helm of the 1963 March on Washington had brushed aside when putting together their landmark event—the traditions of inclusive and horizontal leadership embodied by figures like Ella Baker and Septima Clark. Over the fifty years between the 1963 March on Washington and the 2017 Women's March, there had been a long, slow shift in the nature of grassroots organizing, away from top-down forms of leadership and traditionally structured organizations and toward more fluid and participatory models. Feminist and feminist-led movements had led the way in this extended process of transformation, favoring small groups and collective forms of decision making as part of a broad critique of male-dominated movements that had left too many ordinary participants feeling silenced, disempowered, or marginalized. These new practices spread from movement to movement over the decades, even as the fortunes of individual causes rose and fell; they proliferated at the same time that organizations with traditional chapter and membership structures were undergoing their steady decline, and national advocacy groups were growing more top-heavy and staff-driven. The decentralized, inclusive models of organizing and leadership pioneered by women like Baker and Clark carried over into many different movement contexts, from the consciousness-raising groups of the early women's liberation movement of the 1970s to the fierce and effective AIDS activism of ACT UP in the 1980s and 1990s. They helped shape the women of color feminism pioneered by groups like the Combahee River Collective in the 1980s, whose insights into the interplay of multiple structures of power paved the way for what is now known as intersectional feminism. They were embraced and refined by such disparate organizing endeavors as the turn-of-the-millennium movement against corporate globalization, the Occupy movement, and Black Lives Matter, all of which eschewed top-down structures and charismatic leadership in favor of more collaborative approaches. As logistics coordinator Janaye Ingram explained, the Women's March organizers embraced a vision of a "'leaderful' movement . . . where there isn't a single person whose vision creates the strategy, but rather many people who can be visionary leaders."[38]

The coordinators of the Women's March offered leadership in two key ways. The first was through political framing—their commitment to placing women of color and an intersectional analysis at the center of the organizing work. The Unity Principles they developed and disseminated for the event spelled out this approach in detail: "We must create a society in which women—including Black women, Native women, poor women, immigrant women, disabled women, Muslim women, lesbian queer and trans women—are free and able to care for and nurture their families, however they are formed, in safe and healthy environments free from structural impediments." The second was by establishing the broad framework that made all the marches possible, creating a political opportunity that others could embrace—and shape. "No one person was responsible for any part of it, but we made the space for it and we made the space possible for it," said Ingram afterward. "Women are tapping into our voices and using our voices in ways that we maybe haven't felt comfortable and empowered to do in the past." It was the example of women stepping up to lead at the national level that inspired so many women to step up at the local level to lead the hundreds of sister marches—and it was the ubiquity of these local events that launched the resistance to Trump with such vigor.[39]

It may be difficult to remember the climate of fear and paralysis that overtook many Americans in the wake of the 2016 election. Throughout the grim stretch between Election Day and the inauguration, the mood was muted in many quarters. Given the scale of the calamity that the country had experienced—the elevation to the presidency of a racist, misogynist, authoritarian buffoon who lost the popular vote and owed his election to factors that raised serious questions of legitimacy—the initial response was strikingly small in scale and muted in character. There were a number of protests in this period, but they were modest in size and rather dispiriting. The biggest crowds in New York in those earliest days rarely exceeded 10,000 or 20,000, and one march, it turned out, wasn't even organized by anti-Trump forces, but rather called by Russian trolls. Hate crimes and bias attacks fostered by Trump's campaign had soared around the country in the weeks surrounding the election, and many people seemed overcome by shock, depression, and fear, spending their days debating how bad things might get and limiting their online communications, whether by installing a private messaging app like Signal, hiding or deleting public accounts, or retreating into private online groups. Planning a major mobilization in this climate was a bold act, one that helped others find the hope they would need to move forward. When women and allies emerged from their stunned state to march all around the

The 1995 Million Man March in Washington, DC, which researchers determined had 837,000 attendees. Photo by Maureen Keating

country on January 21, they were reclaiming their voices and the public and political space for action in the very act of marching. The low-tech medium of the do-it-yourself sign proved to be a deeply satisfying and powerful part of that process, but it was the larger tactic of the mass protest march—the direct, bodily experience of assembling in large numbers and acting in concert—that broke the nationwide spell of fear and silence.[40]

In the decades since the 1963 March on Washington, mass mobilizations had very quickly gone from a daring and novel form of political expression to a mainstay of dissent in America, repeated time and time again. First came a series of national protests against the Vietnam War in 1965, 1967, and 1969—big convergences organized by broad coalitions of peace and social justice organizations. This was a period in American history when numerous new social movements were emerging, and as movements proliferated, so did marches. Feminist, antinuclear, and lesbian and gay marches followed in the 1970s, while a series of DC mobilizations in the 1980s brought sizable showings by organized labor, pro-choice feminists, and advocates of lesbian and gay rights, among others. Holding a national march became a way for a movement to confirm and solidify its presence as a political force. The marches served as important touchstones for their respective movements, even if none of these subsequent events was ever viewed as having the stature of the 1963 March on Washington. By the 1990s, hardly a year passed without a major march in Washington, some so enormous that they dwarfed the 1963 event in size, like the 1993 March on Washington for Lesbian, Gay and Bi Equal Rights and Liberation and the 1995 Million Man March led by Louis Farrakhan, the controversial head of the Nation of Islam. (The Million Man March was not a traditional protest—much of its focus was on collective self-help and

MARCHING ON WASHINGTON:
MAJOR PROTESTS IN THE US CAPITAL, 1963–2017

DATE	EVENT	ATTENDANCE
1963 (Aug. 28)	March on Washington for Jobs and Freedom (civil rights)	250,000
1969 (Nov. 15)	National Mobilization to End the War (Vietnam War)	500,000
1970 (May 9)	Protest of Cambodia Invasion/Kent State Shooting (Vietnam War)	150,000
1971 (Apr. 24)	Vietnam War Out Now Rally	500,000
1979 (Oct. 14)	National March on Washington for Lesbian and Gay Rights	75,000
1981 (Sept. 19)	Solidarity Day (organized labor)	250,000
1983 (Aug. 27)	20th Anniversary March on Washington (civil rights)	250,000
1986 (Mar. 9)	March for Women's Lives (pro-choice)	100,000
1987 (Oct. 11)	Second National March on Washington for Lesbian and Gay Rights	650,000
1987 (Dec. 6)	March for Soviet Jewry	250,000
1989 (Apr. 9)	March for Women's Lives (pro-choice)	150,000
1989 (Nov. 12)	Mobilize for Women's Lives (pro-choice)	225,000
1992 (Apr. 5)	March for Women's Lives (pro-choice)	600,000
1993 (Apr. 25)	March on Washington for Lesbian, Gay and Bi Equal Rights and Liberation	800,000
1995 (Oct. 16)	Million Man March (Black male empowerment)	837,000
2000 (Apr. 30)	Millennium March for Equality (LGBTQ)	500,000
2000 (May 14)	Million Mom March (gun control)	500,000
2004 (Apr. 25)	March for Women's Lives (pro-choice)	1,000,000
2005 (Sept. 24)	March to End the War in Iraq	200,000
2017 (Jan. 21)	Women's March on Washington	800,000

Black male empowerment—but it was clearly an oppositional gathering.) The big mobilizations were punctuated by many smaller ones, but gauging and comparing any of them by size became more difficult after the huge 1995 convergence. Heated disputes over whether or not a million people had indeed marched at the Million Man March led Congress to end the National Park Service's practice of issuing official crowd estimates, figures that appeared neutral but had clearly been manipulated for political reasons, both on this occasion and in the past. (In the end, a team of researchers from Boston University analyzed aerial photographs of the event and came up with a crowd size of 837,000—shy of a million, but still one of the largest DC marches ever, and more than double the National Park Service estimate of 400,000.) Even with the uncertainty built into assessing crowd sizes, it's safe to say that more than two dozen protest marches with more than 100,000 participants took place in Washington in the five decades after the 1963 mobilization, or at least one major march every other year. Marching on Washington was the emblematic way to hold a major protest, and a way for movements to make a bid for national standing, but the model also quickly spread to other major cities like New York and Los Angeles, where mass transit facilitated mass mobilization. Four of the ten largest demonstrations in US history took place outside DC, including a landmark 1982 nuclear disarmament protest in New York, which may have topped 1 million attendees, and an enormous 2006 day of action for immigrant rights in Los Angeles, which brought at least 650,000 people into the streets.[41]

One reason big protest marches so quickly became a standard feature of American political life is that people viewed them as a powerful way to exercise political pressure, thanks in part to how they understood the

MASS MOBILIZING: THE TEN LARGEST PROTEST EVENTS IN US HISTORY

DATE	EVENT	LOCATION	ATTENDANCE
1982	March and Rally for Peace and Disarmament (anti-nuclear)	New York	1,000,000
1987	Second National March on Washington for Lesbian and Gay Rights	Washington, DC	650,000
1992	March for Women's Lives (pro-choice)	Washington, DC	600,000
1993	March on Washington for Lesbian, Gay and Bi Equal Rights and Liberation	Washington, DC	800,000
1995	Million Man March (Black male empowerment)	Washington, DC	837,000
2004	March for Women's Lives (pro-choice)	Washington, DC	1,000,000
2004	"World Says No to the Bush Agenda" March at the Republican National Convention	New York	800,000
2006	May 1 Immigrant Rights Protest	Los Angeles	650,000
2017	Women's March	Washington, DC	800,000
2017	Women's March	Los Angeles	650,000

1963 March on Washington. This, it turned out, was its own myth: Mass marches simply haven't worked very well as a pressure tactic. When you look closely at the dozens of mobilizations modeled after the 1963 march, it's hard to find any with a concrete, near-term legislative or policy impact. A 1978 march for the Equal Rights Amendment did succeed in the narrow goal of spurring Congress to extend the deadline for the measure's ratification, but the ERA itself never passed. A major pro-choice march in 1989, meanwhile, failed to persuade the Supreme Court to rule in favor of abortion rights in the major case then before it, *Webster v. Reproductive Health*. On some occasions, when the administration in office was sympathetic to the cause but needed more prodding to take action, mobilizing large crowds into the streets seemed to have an effect. One of the most notable examples was not a classically left-wing mobilization, but a 1987 demonstration in Washington on the rights of Soviet Jews that drew some 250,000 participants and pushed President Ronald Reagan to take a stronger stance in negotiations with Soviet Premier Mikhail Gorbachev. Mass marches targeting hostile administrations—whether the antiwar marches of the late 1960s or the pro-choice marches of the Reagan and Bush years—set a larger political tone and kept dissent alive and visible, but in policy terms, they could feel like shouting into the void. They may indeed have made a more solid and lasting contribution than that, but their impact is impossible to measure: Who can know how much longer the Vietnam War might have continued had it not been met by mass protests, or gauge how much greater the erosion of women's reproductive freedom under Reagan and Bush might have been without sustained pro-choice mobilization? Some big protests, such as the Solidarity Day march, a 1981 mobilization spearheaded by the AFL-CIO just as the labor movement was facing years of attacks and decline under the Reagan and Bush administrations, seemed inadvertently to demonstrate how little real power the gathered forces actually had, but that didn't mean they weren't worth organizing as a way of holding ground. The notion that mass protests must lead to short-term policy change in order to be effective misses all the other kinds of impact they can have. There is, in fact, only one march in American history that can be unambiguously described as having successfully worked as an immediate pressure tactic, and it's the one that didn't happen: the 1941 march planned by A. Philip Randolph, which represented such a powerful threat to the wartime administration of Franklin Delano Roosevelt that it pushed him to issue his landmark executive order barring racial discrimination in defense industries.[42]

The 1963 March on Washington had, after all, established a certain character for the mass mobilization in America: huge—often impressively so—but fundamentally and emphatically unthreatening to those in power. Roosevelt had found the prospect of large Black crowds marching on the nation's capital so dangerous and unnerving in 1941 that he acquiesced to organizers' demands in order to keep it from happening: He feared a popular uprising on his doorstep. John F. Kennedy's artfully accommodating approach twenty-two years later, coupled with A. Philip Randolph and Bayard Rustin's commitment to discipline and order, had removed any whiff of insurrection from the March on Washington, and that quality carried over into the many marches that followed in its footsteps. Paradoxically, what might seem on the surface (and to FDR) like one of the most militant tools in the organizer's toolbox—the amassing of huge crowds to make political demands—became, as practiced in the United States, one of the mildest. To ensure the broadest possible participation, organizers would in almost every case negotiate with the authorities to secure a permit, a process that could often constrain the protest's character and impact, much as when the Kennedy administration maneuvered the organizers of the March on Washington into accepting a far more anodyne staging of the event than they had initially intended. Sometimes the permitting process was so onerous it altered the character of a protest entirely, as for instance when the New York Police Department refused to allow protesters to hold a march on February 15, 2003, the day of the huge anti–Iraq War protests around the world. Demonstrators were only given permission to hold a stationary rally, and were surrounded with metal pens, which both seriously undermined the basic right to public assembly and created hazardous conditions for participants.[43]

There have certainly been numerous sizable protests in American history for which no one sought the authorities' advance permission. From the 1999 blockade of the World Trade Organization meetings in Seattle, where demonstrators disrupted a major trade summit as a protest against corporate attacks on human rights and the environment, to the nationwide Occupy protests of 2011 decrying economic inequality, to the Black Lives Matter marches against police brutality and impunity in 2014 and 2015, direct-action-oriented movements have typically shunned police permits, preferring to negotiate the terms of a protest as it's under way. These events, though, have rarely attracted more than 25,000 or 50,000 participants; the greater risks involved in protesting without official permission have meant that even the largest direct actions in American history have

Protesters corralled into pens at the February 15, 2003, rally against the Iraq War in New York. Demonstrators had been denied permission to hold a march. Photo by Garth Liebhaber

involved substantially smaller numbers than the average permitted mass march. Every single demonstration in American history with more than 100,000 participants has been, to a greater or lesser degree, sanctioned and shaped by authorities, and nearly every one has played by the established rules. With only one exception, during the height of Vietnam antiwar protests in 1970, the huge crowds that converged in Washington for mass demonstrations never once left their preapproved march routes to, say, storm the halls of Congress or mount a surprise sustained occupation of the White House grounds. These giant events have been occasions for marchers to express their views in a peaceful and circumscribed way and then go home. Big marches might feel like a form of collective direct action, when you're there in the midst of a huge crowd with shared purpose—a scaling-up of tactics like sit-ins and blockades. But that's mostly not how they function. They're less about wielding power than about gathering it.

The fact that mass marches haven't worked very well as a pressure tactic is of course one reason why skeptics question whether protests work at all. But movements are complex, as are the mechanisms through which they grow, exercise influence, and sustain themselves over time. "I wish it was that easy to get policy changed by having a march or a civil disobedience, but we have come to appreciate that the process of change is a lot more complicated," comments Leslie Cagan, who has played a central role in many of the largest demonstrations in American history. (Cagan was either the overall coordinator or on the top leadership team for the 1982 nuclear disarmament march in New York, the 1987 March on Washington for Lesbian and Gay Rights, the 2003 "World Says No to War" mobilization against the war in Iraq, the 2004 protest outside the Republican National Convention in New York, and the 2014 People's Climate March.) "Virtually

The 1979 National March on Washington for Lesbian and Gay Rights. Photo by Bettye Lane

all the tactics we use are just steps in a process and not the culmination of a process," she notes. "If they're done well, they lead to other steps."[44]

The mass mobilization, over time, became most important not for leveraging power, but for building movements, solidifying the commitment of participants and helping movements gain the followers and recognition they need to create change in the longer term. Mass demonstrations give participants a palpable sense of belonging to something bigger than themselves; they provide validation of a movement's existence and persistence. Their scale of course sends an important signal to legislators and policymakers, but in some ways it sends an even more important one to participants and sympathetic or interested observers. Mass protests, as they have been used in the United States, don't so much harness power as galvanize the hope upon which organizing depends, opening up political space for further, and more targeted, action. They are occasions for groups and movements to converge and cross-fertilize, for individuals to plug into an array of ongoing initiatives and campaigns, and for everyone, including outside observers, to see the range and scale of forces behind a cause. Their mild character invites broad participation, making everyone from elders to families with small children feel safe attending. Ideally, as Cagan puts it, they "serve as an on-ramp for people who have never stepped out or stepped up in a public way." Those who join a mass march and then go home contribute something by showing up, to be sure—the work of social and cultural change sometimes proceeds through means as modest as somebody telling their friends about the big march they went to—but the longer-term impact of a large-scale protest lies in what other actions it inspires. Movement work is almost always a marathon, and mass demonstrations help keep movements going.[45]

This quality helps explain why repetition has been a hallmark of the mass mobilization in America. Numerous movements have chosen to march on Washington over and over again, as a way of sustaining their identity and momentum. There were two sizable commemorations of the 1963 March on Washington, for instance: a major twentieth anniversary event in 1983 and a fiftieth anniversary gathering in 2013, while Barack Obama occupied the White House. Lesbian, gay, bisexual, and transgender activists have marched on Washington multiple times, with each gathering serving as a kind of milestone for the larger movement and a marker of its evolution. When lesbians and gay men first converged in Washington for a mass march in 1979, the simple fact of gathering in large numbers in the nation's capital was a daring step, a powerful and very public form of coming out, deeply affecting both for those who marched and for many who watched them. The formal demands of that event, including a call for comprehensive federal gay and lesbian rights legislation, remain mostly unmet. (Presidents Clinton and Obama did issue executive orders in 1998 and 2014 banning discrimination in federal employment based on sexual orientation or identity, but a 2017 executive order by Donald Trump weakened those provisions.) Yet it's abundantly clear that marching then—and again in 1987, 1993, and 2009—helped give the LGBTQ movement both visibility and legitimacy, welcoming new waves of participation into the cause. It would be too simplistic to credit any of these marches with, say, the 2015 Supreme Court ruling that legalized same-sex marriage nationwide, and the more recent ones have tended to be bland and corporate-dominated affairs, but they have clearly functioned as important components of a long process of social and cultural change.

The paradox, though, is that the mobilizations that help sustain broad movements often deplete the groups that organize them. The exhaustion that many organizers felt after the 1963 March on Washington was not an anomaly; all too often, those who do the work of putting a big protest together are simply too drained by the effort to provide clear and effective ways to build on the collective outpouring, at least right away. The perception that big marches come and go like the weather often rests on the fact that the organizers of any given protest typically lack the capacity or energy to implement immediate next steps, much as the sponsoring groups for the 1963 March on Washington were simply too worn out from the mobilizing process to do much of anything with the tens of thousands of pledge cards gathered from the crowd. Frequently it's the initiatives that spin off from a mobilization that best carry the work forward in the near term. National Coming Out Day, for instance, was first held to commemorate the 1987 March on Washington for Lesbian and Gay Rights and extend its contribution; it's now an annual event marked in communities all around the country. If movements are marathons, mass protests function somewhat like relay stations: To keep the momentum going, the torch often needs to pass into new hands.

This arena is where the experience of the 2017 Women's Marches proved most distinctive, and most unlike previous mass demonstrations in America. The self-mobilizing that enabled them to come together so quickly and powerfully led directly into new forms of self-organizing in their wake. The bottom-up and do-it-yourself character of the marches, so evident in all those handmade signs, carried over into the nascent resistance to Trump, as did the feminist traditions of inclusive and collaborative leadership. The fact that there were so many sister marches all around the country and the work of putting them together was so decentralized meant that no single organization or set of organizations became depleted and exhausted by the effort. A great many participants left the marches feeling energized, and they channeled that energy into a remarkable array of grassroots organizing work.

There's an academic study of the Tea Party that has become famous among social movement scholars for the way it illuminates the lasting impact a single protest gathering can have. The Tea Party emerged as a nationwide network of conservative groups in response to the election of President Barack Obama; it took many of its organizing cues from historic movements of the left and had genuine grassroots support, but it was also heavily funded and steered over time by powerful right-wing figures, including the billionaires David and Charles Koch. The researchers looked closely at weather and attendance during a coordinated nationwide day of Tea Party rallies on Tax Day in 2009. There were about five hundred of these events nationwide, a quite impressive number. Some happened under fair skies and enjoyed good-sized attendance, while rain kept people away from others. Using sophisticated data analysis, the studies' authors were able to show that in places where the weather didn't inter-fere, the local Tea Party movement was stronger and more influential over time than in places where the Tax Day rallies were rained out, with signifi-cant impacts on everything from how their representatives voted on pend-ing legislation to voter turnout in subsequent elections. The study confirms something many organizers intuitively know but have been hard-pressed to prove concretely: The way that a single protest event unfolds can affect the whole shape and power of a movement going forward. A good part of that impact depends on the skill of the organizers, the resonance of their cause, and the strength of the opposition, but some of it is a matter of chance, like happening to have good weather on the day a demonstration is scheduled.[46]

For the emerging resistance to Trump, it would matter deeply that the local Women's Marches were so numerous and so well attended, that they came together in such a viral and nontraditional way, and that the marchers, with all their many signs, were not an audience but the main event. The DC Women's March anchored the nationwide mobilization, but it wasn't central in the same way that previous big marches on Washington had been: The vitality and scale of the 650 sister marches transformed the overall experience of the day. Movements had organized nationwide days of local protest many times in the past, going back at least to the October 1969 Moratorium to End the War in Vietnam, when millions took part in coordinated antiwar activities all around the United States, but typically these kinds of protests involved only about 200 cities. These distributed protests had, moreover, almost always been called or coordinated by a single organization or coalition—for instance, United for Peace and Justice spearheaded some 235 local protests around the country to coincide with its big New York antiwar rally on February 15, 2003. In 2017, by contrast, there was a spontaneous and insurgent character to the whole undertaking, with many people who had not been politically active before, most of them women, stepping up to organize local events, often in communities where protests had rarely happened. New leaders emerged in places large and small, bringing to life that deeply democratic vision of Septima Clark's—the one that Dr. King and his colleagues had once found laughable. Perhaps the most distinctive quality of protest as the Trump era unfolded was how ubiquitous it was. The stunning nationwide reach of

MARCHING EVERYWHERE:
THE LARGEST COORDINATED PROTESTS IN US HISTORY

DATE	PROTEST	LOCATIONS AND ATTENDANCE
October 1969	Moratorium to End the War in Vietnam	• Antiwar actions in 200+ cities • More than 2 million participate in a range of activities, from teach-ins to demonstrations
May 1970	Nationwide Student Strike against the War	• Demonstrations, walkouts, and shutdowns at 1,000+ college campuses • An estimated 4 million directly affected by actions (a much smaller number directly participate in protests)
February 2003	"World Says No to War" Protests	• Antiwar demonstrations in 235+ US cities, with many more around the globe • An estimated 1 million Americans participate
March–May 2006	Immigrant Rights Protests	• Strikes, walkouts, and major protests in 140+ cities over the course of two months • At least 4 million participate
January 2017	Women's Marches	• Protests in 650+ cities • At least 4.2 million participate
January 2018	Women's Marches	• Protests in 400+ cities • At least 2.2 million participate
March 2018	Student Walkouts on Gun Violence	• Students walk out of 4,470+ schools • At least 1.4 million participate
March 2018	March for Our Lives	• Rallies and marches against gun violence in 765+ cities • At least 1.8 million participate

the 2017 Women's Marches set a new pattern for coordinated protest mobilization in the United States. In the year and a half after those initial post-inauguration actions, decentralized protests proliferated, touching a record number of communities throughout the United States.[47]

One year into the toxic presidency, there would be almost ten local resistance groups for every Women's March that had happened in January 2017—a total of 6,000 groups, which is vastly more than, say, the 800 to 1,000 local groups that the Tea Party could boast at its height. Some of this work was directly catalyzed by the national organizing team of the Women's March. Among the action steps they offered in the wake of the big mobilization was a call to form small "huddles," a number of which evolved into ongoing resistance groups. The Women's March national team also worked after the 2017 event to build a traditionally structured national organization with formal chapters, and some solid organizing happened in this way, but this wasn't where the biggest wave of energy went. Instead, there was a relay effect: The largest hub for resistance activity in the year following the marches was the loose network coordinated by Indivisible, an organization started by former Democratic congressional staffers eager to share what they had learned from observing how the Tea Party had leveraged grassroots pressure during the Obama years. Indivisible offered tools and guidance to their affiliate groups, but did so in a way that acknowledged and celebrated local autonomy. "We're not the leaders of this movement: you are," declared the tagline at the head of Indivisible's website. When the network was not quite one year old, Leah Greenberg, one of Indivisible's cofounders, described being struck by "just the sheer range of different kinds of work that [local groups] are doing and different approaches they've taken, based on who started the group and where they are and the geographic and political context." Many groups focused strongly on the specific kinds of congressional advocacy outlined in the Indivisible Guide, flooding their representatives' town hall meetings and inundating their offices with coordinated phone calls. Many also emphasized grassroots electoral work, from registering voters to supporting local candidates for office to canvassing door-to-door. But groups took up many other types of activism as well. Some organized direct support for members of their community targeted by immigration enforcement or mounted campaigns around issues such as fossil-fuel pipeline construction, sexual assault and harassment, gun control, or the removal of local symbols of white supremacy. Resistance groups tended to be both multi-issue and multi-tactical.[48]

There were many political challenges associated with the sprawling, networked character of the resistance and the small-d democratic organizing visions it embraced. To outside observers, the proliferation of groups and approaches could be baffling—a movement without a charismatic leader or a single organizational container isn't easy to read. (A writer for the *New York Times Magazine* called them "inchoate volunteer armies" in a long, head-scratching piece about their highly effective role in Virginia's November 2017 elections: "They were hard to keep track of: who was with which group, what each one cared about, which groups were subgroups or affinity groups of other groups, which had national umbrella organizations and which didn't, which terms of art groups preferred to describe their particular variety of leaderlessness.") This decentralized style of organizing may or may not work better than more centralized approaches—it's both vibrant and unwieldy—but it's the kind of activism that has attracted the most adherents in recent times. People vote with their feet when they join movements, and they've tended to vote for ones where they have a strong sense of voice and autonomy.[49]

There was a noteworthy tension between that desire for autonomy and the question of political accountability—the intersectional principle of taking leadership from those most affected by injustice. While women of color stepped up to provide leadership for the national Women's March and in numerous local resistance groups, the new groups that formed after the election tended to be whiter than the population at large. They were not just mostly women, but in many cases, disproportionately white women. Resistance organizing in communities of color was more often anchored in groups that predated the election, many of them with long histories of solid grassroots work. The new wave of activism represented both an opportunity to swing white voters away from the Trump agenda, especially white women voters, and a potential hurdle in organizing a genuinely progressive and intersectional movement, for many of these white women had little experience directly addressing the racism that was central to Trump's popular appeal. There are, it's worth recalling, robust traditions of grassroots organizing by white women in the service of white supremacy. White women were crucial to the mobilizing and movement-building work of groups ranging from the Ku Klux Klan of the 1920s to the John Birch Society of the 1950s to the Tea Party of the Obama era. A key political project for the resistance writ large was continuing to work through the issues of race and racism that came to the surface during the initial organizing of the Women's Marches.[50]

Part of the power of the Women's Marches was that they never even pretended to be about applying direct pressure on the new president. They were sending a different kind of signal. The trajectory of movements is long and slow and complex. Protests do sometimes force direct concessions—smaller, sustained, targeted ones do so more effectively than mass mobilizations—but that's far from the only way they can be effective. Organizing isn't a science—it's an art. When the odds are against you, protests can shift the terms of public debate or expand the sense of what's politically possible. They can motivate people on the sidelines to step up and take action. They can put an issue on the agenda, or increase the urgency with which it is addressed. They introduce friction where injustice depends on the illusion of harmony. The work that protests do often can't be seen in the moment. Their effects tend to be subtle, dispersed, and catalytic. There are occasions, of course, when you're destined to lose whatever it is you're fighting for, and a protest is just a cry of frustration. But other times the arc of history does bend toward justice, and there are magical moments when—often quite suddenly—you win. Protesting is always an act of faith, a gamble that action might spark more action, that inspiration will travel in unpredictable ways, that taking a bold public stand will set new forces into motion, that justice will prevail. Perhaps the biggest challenge that movements face is sustaining the hope that's required for people to keep taking action over time. So sometimes the most consequential way a mass protest can work is by changing the protesters themselves, giving them the taste of collective power they need to stay in the fight.

Protest against the Muslim ban gets underway at John F. Kennedy Airport, New York, January 2017. Photo by L.A. Kauffman

Some protests come together so quickly that no one has time to prepare signs. That's what happened one week after the 2017 Women's Marches, when Donald Trump's new administration announced a ban on travelers from Iraq, Syria, Iran, Libya, Somalia, Sudan, and Yemen. Immigrant rights organizers in New York sent out a flurry of text messages to their networks, and protesters immediately began to converge on New York's John F. Kennedy Airport. Initially, there weren't any signs there, just a few dozen protesters huddled on a bleak patch of concrete between the main international terminal and the parking garage. A couple of people thought to bring poster board and markers. Murad Awawdeh, an organizer with the New York Immigration Coalition who helped spearhead the action, leaned over a garbage can and hastily scrawled "Let them IN!" on a sign; other protesters followed suit. As word of the protest spread on social media, the crowd grew rapidly over the course of the day, reaching into the thousands. The new arrivals brought some signs with them, including dramatic lighted signs from the NYC Light Brigade, but overall, the spontaneity of the gathering was reflected in the raggedness of its appearance. It was, and looked like, a major, peaceful uprising. Images of the protest in New York inspired people in dozens of communities around the country to rush to airports in their area for similar impromptu demonstrations. Every major airport in the United States, from Atlanta and Boston to Chicago, Dallas–Ft. Worth, and Los Angeles, witnessed immigrant rights protests that day. "Folks were activated in a way that I've never seen before, to actually show up," Awawdeh later recalled. "And it wasn't people who have always gone to protests or people who always believed in a fair immigration policy or practice. It was people who just felt like what was happening was wrong, and they couldn't stand by and let it happen." The nationwide outpouring sent an extraordinary signal of support for immigrant rights and resistance to the new regime. When court after court ruled against the president's efforts to keep Muslims out of the country in that period, there was a sense in which they were aligning with the sentiment in the streets.[51]

Uprisings are rare, at least in the United States. When spontaneous protests have happened, they have usually arisen from popular frustration so great it cannot be contained, and they have tended to take the form of riots. America has a long tradition of rioting—say, when white neighborhoods have wanted to keep Black families from moving in, or when college basketball teams win championships. Riots born of anger at injustice have, like these others, typically had no formal leaders, no structure, no

Muslim ban protest at John F. Kennedy Airport swells into the thousands, January **2017.** Photo by Lucky Tran

strategy, no rules. Only on very rare occasions have popular upsurges that began with the disorderly character of a riot evolved into something more organized and intentional. The Stonewall riots, which grew out of spontaneous resistance to a June 1969 police raid on an LGBTQ bar, are one noteworthy case. The most striking recent example was in Ferguson, Missouri, after the police killing of Michael Brown in August 2014, where new leadership emerging from the street protests joined forces with seasoned organizers from long-standing local groups and the nationwide Black Lives Matter network to build a sustained movement for police accountability. Much more frequently, these outbursts of popular anger erupt and then fade as soon as authorities restore order, leaving no movements or organized activism in their wake.

The United States has never witnessed the kind of mass political uprising that characterized, say, the Arab Spring, when vast crowds converged on public spaces in Tunisia, Egypt, and other countries beginning in late 2010, calling for fundamental change and ultimately bringing down multiple regimes. Scholars Erica Chenoweth and Maria J. Stephan have studied uprisings like this throughout history and have found that sustained nonviolent resistance by just 3.5 percent of a country's population is enough to dislodge an authoritarian government. It's a remarkable statistic, one that can make major change seem well within reach. When you map it onto the American experience, though, the figure seems anything but small and attainable: That would equal more than 11 million Americans in the streets. It's more than double the highest estimate for the number of protesters who marched all around the United States at the 2017 Women's Marches, as well as more than twice the size of the largest single public gathering in American history, which wasn't a political event at all, but the parade celebrating the Chicago Cubs' 2016 World Series victory. Chenoweth and Stephan's research makes it clear that protest on this scale only topples governments, moreover, when it's sustained, not when it's a single day of action.[52]

But the math of protest, and of movements, is tricky. Short of bringing about regime change, size and impact don't necessarily correlate. Small protests have often achieved more in the way of immediate results than big ones, and the lasting significance of the largest ones has not always been easy to see. Perhaps nothing could have halted the Bush Administration's rush to war with Iraq in 2003, when millions marched all around the globe—a million of them in the United States—in the largest day of protest in world history. After all, a military empire is no small thing to stop. At the time, it seemed galling that George W. Bush simply shrugged the outcry off: "Size of protest—it's like deciding, well, I'm going to decide policy based on a focus group," he declared. As it happened, there was precedent for exactly this sort of bravado when faced with massive opposition in the streets. Richard Nixon had responded in nearly the same way after what were, at that point, the largest protests in American history, the October 1969 Vietnam Moratorium actions that involved some 2 million people all around the country. The protests inspired Nixon's famous "silent majority" speech, in which he claimed that all the people *not* marching represented the true face of American democracy. It was partly a bluff, of course, but Nixon only became truly rattled when the protests against the war grew not just larger but also stronger—when thousands mounted, or tried to mount, the kinds of disruptive nonviolent resistance actions that had typically been organized by small groups of 10 or 50 or 100 and used against smaller targets. In 2003, outside of the San Francisco Bay Area, there were no mass civil disobedience actions against the Iraq War like the audacious Mayday 1971 direct action against the Vietnam War, where tens of thousands of protesters tried to shut down the federal government through nonviolent blockades. Tactical militancy of that sort simply wasn't the temper of the times in 2003, when the long shadow of the 9/11 terror attacks had still left a chill over dissent in America. Marching was as bold as most of those worldwide protests ever got; in New York, that didn't even happen, as protesters acceded to the government's insistence that they only hold a rally.[53]

The impact of a protest comes from a complicated equation, involving not just the number of participants, but the character of the action, the vulnerability of the target, and the ability of the underlying movement to persist and build beyond a single mobilization. The internet has, without a doubt, made it easier to summon large crowds on short notice than it was when mass protests began in America back in 1963, which in turn has made size alone matter less than ever. The large permitted protests that have become regular features of American life can accomplish many things, from changing public opinion to putting lawmakers on notice, but no matter how massive they are, they don't signal a threat to the existing order. The crucial question for big demonstrations, more often than not, is not how many people attend, but what they do—or don't do—afterward.[54]

There was, it must be said, an unmistakable hint of uprising to the Women's Marches, from the democratic and decentralized way they came together to the way they spilled over the spaces intended to contain them. They had been permitted by the authorities, but they felt exuberant and improvised, less like reenacting established rituals of protest than staking out unpredictable new political ground. In Washington,

Protesters outraged by the US invasion of Cambodia hold a sit-in next to a bus being used to barricade the **White House, May 9, 1970.** Photo by Ken Love

DC, although organizers had lined up some 1,500 marshals to help direct the crowds and were ultimately able to engineer a formal step-off to the march, the convergence was so large that it overwhelmed this infrastructure and marchers mostly directed themselves. In a marked contrast to the 1963 march, the bulk of the crowd couldn't see or hear the program on the stage; instead, they engaged with one another, taking in the messages on one another's signs and marveling at just how many people had shown up to march that day. As streams of women and their allies flowed all through the city, feeling empowered by the day's events and with the future unwritten before them, it was tantalizing to imagine what might have happened had they simply decided to stay, surrounding the White House and shutting down the city in a collective refusal to accept the legitimacy of an election in which the losing candidate had won the popular vote and the winner had prevailed only thanks to gerrymandering, voter suppression, an influx of dark money, and foreign meddling. The mood was right; it might have taken only a few well-placed tactical teams to organize the restless crowds to stick around, say, for the duration of the day and evening—staging an impromptu nonviolent blockade just long enough to pose an added challenge to the new presidency and set an even fiercer tone of resistance going forward.

Only one spontaneous occupation like that ever came close to happening in American history, in a nearly forgotten moment of drama at the peak of protests against the Vietnam War. After Richard Nixon announced his invasion of Cambodia at the end of April 1970, huge demonstrations immediately erupted all around the country. When National Guardsmen shot and killed four unarmed demonstrators at one of these, at Kent State University, the protests spread to nearly 1,350 college campuses, impacting some 4 million students nationwide. "The nation was witnessing what amounted to a virtual general and uncoordinated strike by its college youth," wrote the *Washington Post* as the protests were under way. With just ten days' notice, the shortest timeline for any sizable DC mobilization, more than 100,000 protesters converged on the nation's capital for a large, ragtag protest on May 9. They didn't get a permit; there wasn't time to go through the formal permitting process. Nixon was so alarmed at the angry influx that he ordered a barricade to be built around the White

House, made from sixty buses parked end to end. The administration also cleverly offered organizers a last-minute permit to hold a rally at the Ellipse, in the hope (well founded, it turned out) that a staged and stationary event would help contain the protesters' energies. Organizers from the antiwar movement's direct-action wing hoped to surround the building with a large-scale civil disobedience action, involving as many as 20,000 participants, but in the chaos of the day and with serious tactical divisions within the movement—heightened by Nixon's deft move with the permit— the action ended up unfocused and uncoordinated. Groups of protesters, mostly white and male, repeatedly tried but failed to breach the barrier, with police macing them when they tried to climb over or crawl under the buses. Some staged impromptu sit-ins beside the perimeter, in a scruffy and short-lived but no doubt unsettling siege.[55]

Nothing at all like that happened the day after Trump took office—neither a raucous occupation like the New Left one of 1970 or some imagined, women-led alternative. Instead, as the day wore on and darkness approached in DC, marchers started placing their homemade protest signs along the fence around the White House—first, just a few, and then whole stacks of them, creating something between a collective art installation and a simulated barricade. And then the protesters went home, as protesters had done after dozens of major demonstrations before them. Some no doubt felt they had now done their part, having contributed their bodies and voices to the momentous gathering. But both at the big DC March and at the hundreds of sister marches all around the country, a noteworthy number of protesters, mostly women, took the day as a call to further action. You could feel it in the determined mood of the crowd, and you could read it in the signs—an intimation of the bottom-up, women-led organizing to come. All around the country, an impressive number of those who marched were galvanized into further action, taking the sense of collective power they felt in the streets and carrying it forward. Back in their local communities, they donated money to progressive organizations and made phone calls—millions of phone calls—to their elected representatives. They joined existing groups and formed thousands of new ones; they took on the unglamorous and often invisible work required to keep those groups going. They showed up for many subsequent protests, both local and national, ensuring that every initiative by the new president was met by loud and visible opposition. They turned out in large numbers for politicians' town hall meetings, and thousands decided to run for office. They registered people to vote, and went canvassing door-to-door for progressive local candidates. The difference was palpable and dramatic. Movements had created big marches many times before, but this time, in a way that was impossible to predict and marvelous to observe, marching created a movement.

ACKNOWLEDGMENTS

I've been protesting, and thinking about protests, for a very long time. I attended my first sizable march in 1982, when I was seventeen years old. Some ten thousand of us converged on the State Capitol in Illinois to push for ratification of the Equal Rights Amendment. The effort failed, but somehow I was left more inspired by the attempt than I was discouraged by the defeat. (Illinois did finally ratify the ERA, in May 2018.) I can't begin to count how many demonstrations I've attended in the decades since that first time I marched, but there have been hundreds.

On numerous occasions I've been a central organizer, and some of those experiences have deeply shaped this book. Beginning in 2003, I was the mobilizing coordinator for a series of major demonstrations against the Iraq War, including the February 15, 2003, rally in New York and a march at the 2004 Republican National Convention that ranks as one of the largest demonstrations ever to take place in the United States. My job was to get the crowds there, so I've experienced firsthand what it's like to organize a massive protest in just two months, and what it takes to bring the better part of a million people together in the streets. I've also pondered at great length just what we accomplished in the process of doing so—after all, we didn't stop the war, though I never doubted we were right to try. I'm so grateful to Leslie Cagan for bringing me onto the staff of United for Peace and Justice back then, and for all she's taught me about organizing over the decades (not to mention her help with numerous specific questions for this project). Much appreciation to the many brilliant organizers I've been lucky enough to work with over the years, in UFPJ and many other contexts: Everything I've learned about organizing has been through collaboration.

Thanks to Dan Fox for commissioning the short essay for *Frieze* that got me thinking about the signs at the 2017 Women's March—and which led me to investigate why the signs at the 1963 March on Washington all looked alike. The New York Public Library's Schomburg Center for Research in Black Culture, the Library of Congress, and George Washington University took special steps to make their archival materials from the 1963 march accessible to me, for which I'm very grateful. A big thank you as well to the Lesbian Herstory Archives and the Swarthmore College Peace Collection for their assistance with photo research. I'm grateful to Mrinalini Chakraborty and Janaye Ingram for taking the time to talk through many dimensions of the 2017 Women's March organizing and logistics with me.

Thanks to Rebecca Solnit for encouraging me to pick up the pen again when I was sure I'd never write another book, and to Marina Sitrin for unflagging support and excellent advice throughout the whole process. I'm very grateful to Sue Higgins, Ron Kates, Jean Kauffman, and Vanessa Roe for providing the extraordinary retreats where I did much of my thinking and writing, and to Laurie Arbeiter, David Holiday, Amanda Huron, and Erica McFarquhar for housing me during research—and protest—visits to Washington, DC. Lucy Barber, Paul Buhle, Chris Dixon, and Marina Sitrin provided very helpful feedback on the manuscript, and Amir Amirani, Paul Buhle, Leslie Cagan, Van Gosse, Donna Gould, Emily Hobson, Jeremy Varon, Deborah Wassertzug, and Jessamyn West generously aided my research. I'm especially grateful to the many photographers whose powerful work is included here, including those whose names have been lost to history.

For other key help with this project, thanks to Charlotte Black, Andrew Boyd, Claire Lehmann, Will Meyer, David Patterson, John Price, Lynn Price, Astra Taylor, Sarah Weinman, the Authors Guild, and the HC. Much gratitude to Ron Kuby for once again having my back.

It has been a huge pleasure and honor to work with the University of California Press on this book. I'm enormously grateful to Niels Hooper for bringing me to the press; his enthusiasm for this project and skillful editorial guidance have been nothing short of wonderful. Much appreciation to Tim Sullivan for the history, context, and engagement that helped seal the deal. Big thanks to the entire team that has worked to bring this book to the world, including Kim Robinson, Kate Warne, Jolene Torr, Alexandra Dahne, and Peter Perez. Special appreciation to Lia Tjandra for the gorgeous cover and interior design; Archna Patel for serving as the cover model; Dore Brown and Lindsey Westbrook for their careful and sensitive editing; Bradley Depew for adroitly handling many critical matters, both small and large; and Mandy Keifetz for the index.

The writing of this book was punctuated by a great deal of marching, organizing, and direct action (plus no small amount of sign- and banner-making)—it was a protest-filled year. Cheers and affection to the many folks I've worked with, marched alongside, and learned from along the way, in a wide array of projects. I've been especially fortunate to collaborate politically with the artist and activist Nan Goldin, and I'm honored and moved that she took my author photograph. My biggest thanks go to my beloved N. and D., for being so generally fabulous and putting up with it all.

A NOTE ON PROTEST NUMBERS

Estimating the size of protests is a notoriously difficult business. People come and go, and the boundaries between spectators and participants are often fluid. The problem is compounded by the fact that protest estimates are typically issued by people with vested, and competing, interests: police (or other official sources) and organizers.

Official crowd estimates are especially unreliable. Governments lie about many matters, and they routinely underestimate—often drastically—the numbers of people who mobilize against them. Back in 1971, for instance, President Richard Nixon successfully persuaded the Washington, DC, police chief to announce that 250,000 marched against the Vietnam War, when the crowd size was probably closer to 500,000. In 1995, the National Park Service declared that 400,000 had attended the Million

Man March; researchers later determined that the figure underestimated attendance by at least half. Sometimes the truth slips out, as it did when a New York Police Department spokesperson inadvertently admitted during a public debate that at least 800,000 people—and not 500,000, as they previously claimed—had attended a major march outside the 2004 Republican Convention.

Estimates by protest organizers tend not to be quite as wildly inaccurate as those issued by official sources, but they, too, should be approached with skepticism. Organizers often inflate protest attendance, usually more out of optimism than a desire to deceive.

The protest numbers cited in this book, in both the text and the charts, are my best guesses based on carefully weighing the available figures for each demonstration. I've consulted multiple news accounts of each event, as well as later assessments by historians and other scholars where available. For protests in the Trump era, I've relied heavily on the data of the Crowd Counting Consortium. In all cases, I've taken into account what I know about the political context and the credibility of the various sources. In numerous instances, I've also factored in my own firsthand observations. Some of the figures I use are widely accepted; others remain intensely contested. Because each number ultimately represents my interpretation of the available evidence, and the sources I've consulted are so voluminous, I have not provided footnotes for the charts. Relative size matters, of course. The overall size of protests has grown in the period from 1963 to 2018, but so too has the US population, expanding from 189 million to 325 million. Though the figures here were determined with care, all should be viewed as very imprecise, giving a general sense of the scale of each event rather than anything resembling an exact count.

NOTES

1. Jeanne Theoharis, *A More Beautiful and Terrible History: The Uses and Misuses of Civil Rights History* (Boston: Beacon, 2018).

2. These earlier marches, and the 1963 march, are discussed in detail in Lucy G. Barber, *Marching on Washington: The Forging of an American Political Tradition* (Berkeley and Los Angeles: University of California Press, 2002). On the Detroit Walk to Freedom, see Peniel E. Joseph, *Waiting 'til the Midnight Hour: A Narrative History of Black Power in America* (New York: Henry Holt, 2006), 75–84; Angela D. Dillard, "Religion and Radicalism: The Reverend Albert B. Cleage, Jr., and the Rise of Black Christian Nationalism in Detroit," in *Freedom North: Black Freedom Struggles outside the South, 1940–1980*, ed. Jeanne F. Theoharis and Komozi Woodard (New York: Palgrave Macmillan, 2003), esp. 166–68.

3. Less than two weeks before the coalition met for the first time, NAACP executive secretary Roy Wilkins publicly fulminated against civil rights groups that "furnish the noise and get the publicity while the NAACP furnishes the manpower and pays the bill." Quoted in Yvonne Ryan, *Roy Wilkins: The Quiet Revolutionary and the NAACP* (Lexington: University Press of Kentucky, 2014), 112.

4. A. Philip Randolph quoted in Taylor Branch, *Parting the Waters: America in the King Years 1954–1963* (New York: Simon and Schuster, 1988), 840. The Kennedy quote, from a "confidential source," is from Thomas Gentile, *March on Washington: August 28, 1963* (Washington, DC: New Day, 1983), 37. Though it's impossible to verify this quotation, it is echoed closely in an interview that researcher Albert E. Gollin conducted with CORE leader James Farmer in 1967; according to Farmer, the position of the Kennedy administration was, "If we can't stop it then let's control it." "Interview with Mr. James Farmer at 165 Park Rd., New York, June 9, 1967," Albert E. Gollin/Bureau of Social Science Research Papers, Schomburg Center for Research in Black Culture, New York Public Library, box 6, folder 5, p. 8 (hereafter "Gollin Papers").

5. "Transcript of the President's New Conference on Foreign and Domestic Matters," *New York Times,* July 18, 1963. "Memorandum, 16 August 1963, to A. Philip Randolph, Director, from Bayard Rustin and Tom Kahn," Bayard T. Rustin Papers, Library of Congress, box 29, folder 15. Transcript of July 11, 1963, meeting between march organizers and police, Gollin Papers, box 1, folder 10, p. 18. On the violence faced by some marchers on their way home, see for example "Shots, Rocks Hit 'Freedom' Buses," *Afro-American,* September 7, 1963; "D.C. Marchers Enroute Home Beaten in Miss.," *Atlanta Daily World,* September 11, 1963.

6. "Meet the Press," NBC News Archive, August 25, 1963. Charles Portis, "Washington March Turns into Civil Rights Festival," *Los Angeles Times,* August 23, 1963. "D.C. Police Enlist 2,500 Extra Men," *Jackson Daily News,* August 23, 1963. "The Longer March to Real Equal Rights," *Life,* August 23, 1963. Also see "Fears of Violence Rise over March," *Austin Statesman,* August 27, 1963; "Washington Gets Jittery over March," *Los Angeles Times,* August 28, 1963.

7. The figures on local demonstrations were compiled by scholar John D'Emilio on the basis of Justice Department reports; see John D'Emilio, *Lost Prophet: The Life and Times of Bayard Rustin* (New York: Free Press, 2003), 344. Thomas Gentile provides a roundup of many local actions in *March on Washington,* 95–100. Contemporary accounts include "Racial Storm Warnings on the Increase," *Newsday,* June 1, 1963; "East, Midwest, and South Plagued by Racial Unrest," *Atlanta Constitution,* July 8, 1963; "The 'Revolution' Spreads All over New York," *New York Amsterdam News,* July 27, 1963. On the specific protests mentioned here, see "261 Held as Savannah Negroes March on Police Headquarters," *New York Times,* June 20, 1963; "Dr. Blake among 283 Held in Racial Rally in Maryland," *New York Times,* July 5, 1963; Don Drake, "Sit-ins Halt Cars at Jones Beach: CORE Tries Spirit of 63 at Jones Beach," *Newsday,* July 5, 1963; "Protest by St. Louis Negroes Blocks School Buses," *New York Times,*

June 8, 1963. *Kiplinger Washington Letter,* July 26, 1963, Walter E. Fauntroy Papers, George Washington University, box 30, folder 4.

8. "State Police Called after N.C. Race Riot," *The Sun* (Baltimore), June 8, 1963. On protests in Northern cities during this period and the early stirrings of Black Power, see Thomas J. Sugrue, *Sweet Land of Liberty: The Forgotten Struggle for Civil Rights in the North* (New York: Random House, 2008), esp. 286–312. On the movement in Cambridge, Maryland, see Peter B. Levy, *Civil War on Race Street: The Civil Rights Movement in Cambridge, Maryland* (Gainesville: University Press of Florida, 2003); Sharon Harley, "'Chronicle of a Death Foretold': Gloria Richardson, the Cambridge Movement, and the Radical Black Activist Tradition," in *Sisters in the Struggle: African American Women in the Civil Rights–Black Power Movement,* ed. Bettye Collier-Thomas and V. P. Franklin (New York and London: New York University Press, 2001), 174–96. The Gentile quote is from Thomas Gentile, *March on Washington,* 119.

9. Transcript of July 11, 1963, meeting between march organizers and police, Gollin Papers, box 1, folder 10, p. 24. Rustin's own typewritten notes from this meeting, archived in the same folder as the official transcript, paraphrase the point in even stronger language: "You can be sure they will be the kind of placards which will preserve order." On how Randolph planned to handle the signs in 1941, see Lucy G. Barber, *Marching on Washington,* 124; David Lucander, *Winning the War for Democracy: The March on Washington Movement, 1941–1946* (Urbana: University of Illinois Press, 2014), 30–31.

10. "Organizing Manual No. 1, March on Washington for Jobs and Freedom, August 28, 1963," Gollin Papers, box 1, folder 10, p. 7. The timing of the manual's mailing was ascertained from a cover letter written by staffer Cleveland Robinson and dated July 19 (Rustin Papers, Library of Congress, box 29, folder 15). Undated and edited draft of second March on Washington Organizing Manual, Rustin Papers, Library of Congress, box 30, folder 1. As an example of how Rustin viewed the lines of authority in the march organizing, he declared during the July 11 police meeting, "This is to be a Non-Violent March and no one except Mr. Wilkins, Rev. King, Mr. James Farmer, Mr. John Lewis, Mr. A. Philip Randolph, and Woodley [*sic*] Young, will make policy for this March, and they will determine the exact details of everything that takes place on the March in Washington" (transcript of July 11, 1963, meeting between march organizers and police, Gollin Papers, box 1, folder 10, p. 4). Thanks to Mari Jo Buhle and Steve Max for the detail about the invention of the Magic Marker.

11. On the process of approving slogans see Charles Euchner, *Nobody Turn Me Around: A People's History of the 1963 March on Washington* (Boston: Beacon, 2010), 110–11; lists

of potential slogans submitted to the National Committee for consideration, including Moe Foner's list, can be found in the Rustin Papers, Library of Congress, box 31, folder 8. The instructions regarding "signs of identification" are from the second and final organizing manual, which is available online: "Final Plans for the March on Washington for Jobs and Freedom, August 28, 1963," http://www.thekingcenter.org/archive/document/final-plans-march-washington-jobs-and-freedom. The limitation on signs of identification is described in "March on Washington, Bulletin #2, 8-19-63, Instructions for Participants from the Washington Area," Walter E. Fauntroy Papers, George Washington University, box 30, folder 12. "Policing picket signs": "Transcript of Interview with Dr. John Morsell, Assistant Executive Secretary, NAACP, Held in Dr. Morsell's Office, New York, June 7, 1967," Gollin Papers, box 6, folder 12, p. 10. Marshal protocol: "March on Washington for Jobs and Freedom, August 28, 1963, Marshals' Manual," Rustin Papers, Library of Congress, box 30, folder 15.

12. Malcolm X, *The Autobiography of Malcolm X* (New York: Random House, 1964), 323, emphasis in original.

13. On the history of YPSL and its place in the left political landscape of the early 1960s, including the role played by YPSL leaders Rachelle Horowitz and Tom Kahn, see Maurice Isserman, *If I Had a Hammer: The Death of the Old Left and the Birth of the New Left* (New York: Basic Books, 1987), esp. 61–64, 199–205; James Miller, *"Democracy Is in the Streets": From Port Huron to the Siege of Chicago* (New York: Simon and Schuster, 1987), 74–76.

14. On the attempt to expand the administrative committee for the march see Jennifer Scanlon, *Until There Is Justice: The Life of Anna Arnold Hedgeman* (New York: Oxford University Press, 2016), 156–57. When interviewed by Albert Gollin in 1967, NAACP official John Morsell cited a 1963 membership figure of 515,000 for the NAACP, but that figure is much higher than other estimates and higher than documented membership levels before and after the march. "Transcript of Interview with Dr. John Morsell," Gollin Papers, box 6, folder 12, p. 44. Other estimates of the NAACP's 1963 membership figures include Yvonne Ryan, *Roy Wilkins,* 159–60; Gerald N. Rosenberg, *The Hollow Hope: Can Courts Bring about Social Change?* (Chicago: University of Chicago Press, 2008), 154; "Mapping NAACP Chapters 1912–1977," Mapping American Social Movements Through the 20th Century, University of Washington, https://depts.washington.edu/moves/NAACP_map-basic.shtml. For NCNW membership figures see Jo Freeman, *A Room at a Time: How Women Entered Party Politics* (Lanham, MD: Rowman and Littlefield, 2000), 137.

15. Septima Clark is quoted in Cynthia Stokes Brown, *Ready from Within: Septima Clark and the Civil Rights Movement* (Trenton: Africa World, 1990), 77–78; the episode is also discussed in Charles M. Payne, *I've Got the Light of Freedom: The Organizing Tradition and the Mississippi Freedom Struggle* (Berkeley and Los Angeles: University of California Press, 1995), 76. "Transcript of Interview with Dr. John Morsell," Gollin Papers, box 6, folder 12, p. 36. Dorothy I. Height, "'We Wanted the Voice of a Woman to Be Heard': Black Women and the 1963 March on Washington," in *Sisters in the Struggle,* 87. On women civil rights activists' frustration with the March on Washington leadership and their efforts to have a woman speaker, also see Rosalind Rosenberg, *Jane Crow: The Life of Pauli Murray* (New York: Oxford University Press, 2017), 266–71.

16. See Melinda Chateauvert, "Organizing Gender: A. Philip Randolph and Women Activists," in *Reframing Randolph: Labor, Black Freedom, and the Legacies of A. Philip Randolph,* ed. Andrew E. Kersten and Clarence Lang (New York: New York University Press, 2015), 163–94. Coretta Scott King quoted in Jeanne Theoharis, *A More Beautiful and Terrible History,* 165.

17. On the importance of Black women's mobilizing work to the civil rights movement overall, see Belinda Robnett, *How Long? How Long?: African-American Women in the Struggle for Civil Rights* (New York and Oxford: Oxford University Press, 1997), esp. 71–97; Jo Ann Gibson Robinson, *The Montgomery Bus Boycott and the Women Who Started It: The Memoir of Jo Ann Gibson Robinson* (Knoxville: University of Tennessee Press, 1987), esp. 43–47. On the male leadership takeover, see Danielle L. McGuire, *At the Dark End of the Street: Black Women, Rape, and Resistance: A New History of the Civil Rights Movement from Rosa Parks to the Rise of Black Power* (New York: Vintage Books, 2010), 103–5. Charles Payne, "Men Led, but Women Organized: Movement Participation of Women in the Mississippi Delta," in *Women in the Civil Rights Movement: Trailblazers and Torchbearers 1941–1965,* ed. Vicki L. Crawford, Jacqueline Anne Rouse, and Barbara Woods (Bloomington and Indianapolis: Indiana University Press, 1993), 1–12.

18. "Interview with Miss Rachelle Horowitz, the Administrative Assistant to Bayard Rustin of the A. Philip Randolph Institute, New York, June 8, 1967," Gollin Papers, box 6, folder 8, p. 21; I have slightly edited the punctuation for clarity.

19. Albert E. Gollin interview with Bayard Rustin, October 26, 1967, Gollin Papers, box 6, folder 14. Rustin did not, however, make the striking point that has often been attributed to him (for instance in Charles Euchner, *Nobody Turn Me Around,* 9): "In my view it was a classic resolution of the problem of how can you keep a crowd from becoming something else. . . . Transform it into an *audience.*" That quote is from the

interviewer, Albert E. Gollin. The handling of the musical entertainment is described in Charles Euchner, *Nobody Turn Me Around,* 107.

20. The sign from Americus is described in Russell Baker, "Capital Is Occupied by a Gentle Army," *New York Times,* August 29, 1963. On James Lee Pruitt and his unauthorized sign see Charles Euchner, *Nobody Turn Me Around,* 110–12. A slightly different version of Pruitt's story can be found in Michael Thelwell, *Duties, Pleasures, and Conflicts: Essays in Struggle* (Amherst: University of Massachusetts Press, 1987), 70–71. William P. Jones cites other examples of unauthorized signs at the march in his history, *The March on Washington: Jobs, Freedom, and the Forgotten History of Civil Rights* (New York and London: W. W. Norton, 2013), 188.

21. The four major studies of the March on Washington—by Thomas Gentile, Lucy Barber, Charles Euchner, and William P. Jones—all feature photographs of the rally, not the march, on their covers. On the sidelining of Coretta Scott King and other women at the march see Taylor Branch, *Parting the Waters,* 880; Jennifer Scanlon, *Until There Is Justice,* 166–67; Jeanne Theoharis, *A More Beautiful and Terrible History,* 169. "Transcript of Interview with Dr. John Morsell," Gollin Papers, box 6, folder 12, p. 13.

22. Michael Thelwell, *Duties, Pleasures, and Conflicts,* 58, 72.

23. On the conflicts over the slogan for the 1965 Fifth Avenue Peace Parade see Nancy Zaroulis and Gerald Sullivan, *Who Spoke Up?: American Protest against the War in Vietnam 1963–1975* (Garden City, NY: Doubleday, 1984), 55–56; Tom Wells, *The War Within: America's Battle over Vietnam* (New York: Henry Holt, 1994), 52–54. The details about the props, buttons, and costumes at the event come from William Borders, "Marchers Are Heckled Here—Eggs and a Can of Paint Are Thrown," *New York Times,* October 17, 1965. On slogans and signs for the 1965 SANE antiwar march in Washington see "Capitol Peace March Drops Plan to Censor Signs," *New York Times,* November 22, 1965; Fred P. Graham, "Vietcong Flags Are Sold in Washington as Groups Arrive for March," *New York Times,* November 26, 1965; as well as Nancy Zaroulis and Gerald Sullivan, *Who Spoke Up?,* 63–64; Tom Wells, *The War Within,* 61. Though no one again tried to control the signs at a protest as completely as organizers did in 1963, conflicts over signage and messaging have been a recurring feature of mass protests. At the 1978 march for the Equal Rights Amendment, for instance, a marshal tried to take away a banner reading "Rites for Lesbian Nation" because it didn't mention the ERA; eventually, she relented and let the marchers keep it. A more vigorous attempt came decades later, in 2006, when organizers of a May 1 immigrant rights rally in Los Angeles asked participants not to wave flags that weren't US flags and took away signs that called for

amnesty. See James Lardner and Neil Henry, "Over 40,000 ERA Backers March on Hill," *Washington Post,* July 17, 1978; Chris Zepeda-Millán, *Latino Mass Mobilization: Immigration, Racialization, and Activism* (Cambridge and New York: Cambridge University Press, 2017), 113.

24. On ACT UP's design practices and their enduring impact on protest aesthetics and organizing, see Douglas Crimp and Adam Rolston, *AIDS Demo Graphics* (Seattle: Bay Press, 1990); Avram Finkelstein, *After Silence: A History of AIDS through Its Images* (Oakland: University of California Press, 2018).

25. On the takedown of ACORN, see Zach Carter and Arthur Delaney, "How the ACORN Scandal Seeded Today's Nightmare Politics," *Huffington Post,* May 5, 2018, https://www.huffingtonpost.com/entry/2009-acorn-scandal_us_5ae23fa6e4b02baed1b86696. Theda Skocpol, *Diminished Democracy: From Membership to Management in American Civic Life* (Norman: University of Oklahoma Press, 2003), 7. INCITE!, ed., *The Revolution Will Not Be Funded: Beyond the Non-Profit Industrial Complex* (Durham, NC: Duke University Press, 2017).

26. Rachelle Horowitz's tally is reproduced in Thomas Gentile, *March on Washington,* 133. The quotations are from "Interview with Miss Rachelle Horowitz," Gollin Papers, box 6, folder 8, pp. 29–31.

27. A reproduction of the March on Washington pledge card, and many other primary sources from the event, can be found at "Pacifism and the American Civil Rights Movement Exhibit," Lillian Goldman Law Library, Yale Law School, https://library.law.yale.edu/pacifism-and-american-civil-rights-movement-exhibit. On the question of movement absorption after mass mobilizations, see Mark Engler and Paul Engler, *This Is an Uprising: How Nonviolent Revolt Is Shaping the Twenty-First Century* (New York: Nation Books, 2016), esp. 75–77.

28. Michael Thelwell, *Duties, Pleasures, and Conflicts,* 72. "Interview with Mr. James Farmer," Gollin Papers, box 6, folder 5, p. 21. On the Queens and St. Louis protests see Will Lissner, "Pickets Chain Themselves to Crane," *New York Times,* September 6, 1963; Caoimhe Ni Dhonaill, "Jefferson Bank: A Defining Moment," Missouri Historical Society, August 26, 2017, http://mohistory.org/blog/jefferson-bank-a-defining-moment/; August Meier and Elliott Rudwick, *CORE: A Study in the Civil Rights Movement, 1942–1968* (Urbana: University of Illinois Press, 1975), 227–38; Thomas Sugrue, *Sweet Land of Liberty: The Forgotten Struggle for Civil Rights in the North* (New York: Random House, 2008), 313–15.

29. The *New York Times* quote comes from Russell Baker, "Capital Is Occupied by a Gentle Army." A recording of "Randolph Reading the Pledge of the March on Washington" is available at https://www.youtube.com/watch?v=M81jv8abnhM.

30. Turnout figures are based on the comprehensive data compiled by the Crowd Counting Consortium, https://sites.google.com/view/crowdcountingconsortium/home. For a summary and overview see Erica Chenoweth and Jeremy Pressman, "This Is What We Learned By Counting the Women's Marches," *Washington Post,* February 7, 2017. I have used a figure for the DC Women's March that is somewhat higher than their best guess, which I believe understates the size of the crowd that day. A figure of 4 million participants is widely cited for the huge nationwide student strike that followed Nixon's Cambodia invasion and the killings at Kent State University in 1970, which would make these events larger as a percentage of population than the Women's Marches, but that figure refers to the number who experienced "significant impact" from the protests, not the substantially lower number who actually participated in them. Richard E. Peterson and John A. Bilorusky, *May 1970: The Campus Aftermath of Cambodia and Kent State* (Berkeley: Carnegie Commission on Higher Education, 1971), 15–27.

31. L.A. Kauffman, "The Trump Resistance Can Best Be Described in One Adjective: Female," *The Guardian,* July 23, 2017; Sarah Kaplan, "A Scientist Who Studies Protest Says 'The Resistance' Isn't Slowing Down," *Washington Post,* May 3, 2017; Jennifer Flynn, "In the Fight to Save Healthcare, the Heroes Ride on Wheelchairs—and Wear Pink," *The Nation,* October 23, 2017.

32. On the poster-making parties, see the Facebook listing for the Anchorage event, http://www.facebook.com/events/640734756127781/, and these news accounts of the others: "Photos: Women Make Posters for March in Tucson and Washington," Tuscon.com, January 6, 2017, http://tucson.com/news/local/photos-women-make-posters-for-march-in-washington-and-tucson/collection_1f6e2b66-d460-11e6-a3c2-5b9d9f476b35.html; Ed Stannard, "New Haven Sign-Makers Prepare for Anti-Trump Marches in Hartford, D.C.," *New Haven Register,* January 13, 2017; Cassie Schirm, "Montanans Prepare for Women's March in Helena with Poster Making Parties," ABCFoxMontana.com, January 20, 2017, http://www.abcfoxmontana.com/story/34311004/montanans-prepare-for-womens-march-in-helena-with-poster-making-parties; Arielle Egozi, "Local Artists Host Community Poster-Making Sessions for Women's March," *Miami New Times,* January 5, 2017. Najeebah Al-Ghadban, "Designer's Note: A Timeline of Events," in *Why I March: Images from the Women's March around the World* (New York: Abrams Image, 2017), 174; the other photo compilation is *Why We March: Signs of Protest and Hope, Voices from the Wom-*

en's March (New York: Artisan Books, 2017). "Women's March Signs Bound for Museums," *Toronto Star,* January 27, 2017.

33. Christopher Mele, "Art Supply Sales Jumped in January, Thanks to Protest Signs, Report Says," *New York Times,* March 22, 2017; for the original, detailed industry report see Leen Nsouli, "Women's Movement Impacts Spending on Office Supplies," NPD Group Blog, https://www.npd.com/wps/portal/npd/us/blog/2017/womens-movement-impacts-spending-on-office-supplies/.

34. Bob Bland quoted in Women's March Organizers and Condé Nast, *Together We Rise: Behind the Scenes at the Protest Heard around the World* (New York: Dey Street, 2018), 37. Telephone interview with Mrinalini Chakraborty, October 2, 2017. On the global trend toward viral, internet-driven protests, see Zeynep Tufekci, *Twitter and Tear Gas: The Power and Fragility of Networked Protest* (New Haven, CT, and London: Yale University Press, 2017), 189–91, 221–22.

35. On the 1997 Million Woman March, see Michael Janofsky, "At Million Woman March, Focus Is on Family," *New York Times,* October 26, 1997; Bobbi Booker, "Million Woman March: 1997 Event Equally Significant," *Philadelphia Tribune,* October 2, 2015. Bland quoted in *Together We Rise,* 37.

36. Women's March Organizers and Condé Nast, *Together We Rise,* 41. Intersectional feminism focuses on the interplay between multiple structures of power, going beyond narrowly gender-based frameworks to explore how white supremacy, heteronormativity, and other forms of domination combine and interact. The term was coined by scholar Kimberlé Crenshaw in 1989. See Kimberlé Crenshaw, "Demarginalizing the Intersection of Race and Sex: A Black Feminist Critique of Antidiscrimination Doctrine, Feminist Theory and Antiracist Politics," *University of Chicago Legal Forum* (1989), http://chicagounbound.uchicago.edu/uclf/vol1989/iss1/8.

37. Telephone interview with Mrinalini Chakraborty, October 2, 2017. Also see Julia Felsenthal, "The Organizers," in Condé Nast Presents, *Rise Up! The Women's Marches around the World* (New York: Condé Nast, 2017), 15–18, 92.

38. I trace this long, slow shift in detail in L.A. Kauffman, *Direct Action: Protest and the Reinvention of American Radicalism* (New York and London: Verso Books, 2017); also see Chris Dixon, *Another Politics: Talking across Today's Transformative Movements* (Berkeley: University of California Press, 2014). On the decline of traditionally structured organizations across this same period, see Theda Skocpol, *Diminished Democracy,* 135–74. On the Combahee River Collective and the origins of intersectional fem-

inism, see Keeanga-Yamahtta Taylor, ed., *How We Get Free: Black Feminism and the Combahee River Collective* (Chicago: Haymarket Books, 2017). Janaye Ingram quoted in Women's March Organizers and Condé Nast, *Together We Rise,* 53.

39. The Women's March Unity Principles can be found at https://www.womensmarch.com/principles/. Telephone interview with Janaye Ingram, February 22, 2018.

40. Ali Breeland, "Thousands Attended Protest Organized by Russians on Facebook," TheHill.com, October 31, 2017, http://thehill.com/policy/technology/358025-thousands-attended-protest-organized-by-russians-on-facebook. For detailed data on the spike in hate crimes and bias incidents, see the Center for the Study of Hate and Extremism report "Hate Crime Analysis & Forecast for 2016/2017," https://csbs.csusb.edu/sites/csusb_csbs/files/Final%20Hate%20Crime%2017%20Status%20Report%20pdf.pdf. Also see Alice Marwick, "A New Study Suggests Online Harassment Is Pressuring Women and Minorities to Self-Censor," *Quartz,* November 24, 2016, https://qz.com/844319/a-new-study-suggests-online-harassment-is-pressuring-women-and-minorities-to-self-censor/.

41. On the 1995 dispute, see Michael Janofsky, "Federal Parks Chief Calls 'Million Man' Count Low," *New York Times,* October 21, 1995. On earlier disputes over crowd size, see "Crowd Counts Differ Greatly," *New York Times,* April 9, 1989. On the change in National Park Service policy on counting crowds, see Jason Alderman, "Here's Why We'll Never Know How Many People Attended the Inauguration," *Huffington Post,* January 20, 2017. On the Boston University crowd count for the Million Man March, see http://www.bu.edu/remotesensing/research/completed/million-man-march/. On the 1982 antinuclear rally, see Paul L. Montgomery, "Throngs Fill Manhattan to Protest Nuclear Weapons," *New York Times,* June 13, 1982. Figures for the 2006 immigrant rights protests are from Xóchitl Bada, Jonathan Fox, and Andrew Selee, eds., *Invisible No More: Mexican Migrant Civic Participation in the United States* (Washington, DC: Woodrow Wilson International Center for Scholars, 2006), 36, https://www.wilsoncenter.org/sites/default/files/Invisible%20No%20More_0.pdf; Irene Bloemraad, Kim Voss, and Taeku Lee, "The Protests of 2006: What Were They, How Do We Understand Them, Where Do We Go?," in *Rallying for Immigrant Rights: The Fight for Inclusion in 21st Century America,* ed. Kim Voss and Irene Bloemraad (Berkeley: University of California Press, 2011), 3–43.

42. See Allison Hoffman, "How We Freed Soviet Jewry," *Tablet Magazine,* December 6, 2012.

43. The NYPD's decision to prohibit a march on February 15, 2003, was upheld by a federal court; see Susan Saulny, "Court Bans Peace March in Manhattan," *New York*

Times, February 11, 2003; New York Civil Liberties Union, *Arresting Protest: A Special Report of the New York Civil Liberties Union on New York City's Protest Policies at the February 15, 2003 Antiwar Demonstration in New York City,* https://www.nyclu.org/sites/default/files/publications/nyclu_pub_arresting_protest.pdf.

44. Telephone interview with Leslie Cagan, October 24, 2017. On the complex ways that movement eruptions influence policy, see Frances Fox Piven, *Challenging Authority: How Ordinary People Change America* (Lanham, MD: Rowman and Littlefield, 2006), 103–8.

45. Telephone interview with Leslie Cagan, October 24, 2017. Art- and poster-making have on occasion been central to bridge building across movements during mass mobilizations. Most notably, the People's Climate Marches of 2014 and 2017 used the process of creating banners, signs, and props to build bridges between different sectors of the movement, especially across lines of race and culture, and to tell the movement's story in a way that rooted it in the communities most affected by climate chaos. See for instance Maayan Cohen, "Art, Climate, and Movement-Building: An Interview with Rachel Schragis," Ace Blog, October 21, 2016, https://acespace.org/blog/interview-rachel-schragis.

46. Daniel Shoag, "Do Political Protests Matter? Evidence from the Tea Party Movement," *Quarterly Journal of Economics* 128, no. 4 (2013): 1633–85.

47. The number of local actions in the United States on February 15, 2003, is taken from the list compiled by United for Peace and Justice at the time of the protests: https://web.archive.org/web/20030801135105/http://www.unitedforpeace.org:80/article.php?id=725.

48. The number of local resistance groups is based on those affiliated with the Indivisible directory, which include many Women's March huddles and other types of groups, not just Indivisible chapters. The number of Tea Party groups is from Theda Skocpol and Vanessa Williamson, *The Tea Party and the Remaking of Republican Conservatism* (Oxford and New York: Oxford University Press, 2012), 22. On the origins of the Indivisible Guide, see Charles Bethea, "The Crowdsourced Guide to Fighting Trump's Agenda," *New Yorker,* December 16, 2016. Telephone interview with Leah Greenberg, October 25, 2017.

49. Gideon Lewis-Kraus, "How the 'Resistance' Helped Democrats Dominate Virginia," *New York Times Magazine,* November 13, 2017.

50. On white women's mobilizing and organizing in the service of white supremacy, see Linda Gordon, *The Second Coming of the KKK: The Ku Klux Klan of the 1920s and the*

American Political Tradition (New York and London: Liveright, 2017), esp. 109–37; Lisa McGirr, *Suburban Warriors: The Origins of the New American Right* (Princeton, NJ: Princeton University Press, 2001); Michelle M. Nickerson, *Mothers of Conservativism: Women and the Postwar Right* (Princeton, NJ: Princeton University Press, 2012); Elizabeth Gillespie McRae, *Mothers of Massive Resistance: White Women and the Politics of White Supremacy* (New York: Oxford University Press, 2018). On women's role in the Tea Party see Theda Skocpol and Vanessa Williamson, *The Tea Party and the Remaking of Republican Conservatism,* 42–44.

51. Telephone interview with Murad Awawdeh, October 27, 2017. Adrienne Mahsa Varkiani, "Here's Your List of All the Protests Happening against the Muslim Ban," *ThinkProgress,* January 21, 2017, https://thinkprogress.org/muslim-ban-protests-344f6e66022e/.

52. Erica Chenoweth and Maria J. Stephan, *Why Civil Resistance Works: The Strategic Logic of Nonviolent Conflict* (New York: Columbia University Press, 2011).

53. Richard W. Stevenson, "Threats and Responses: The White House; Protests Fail to Sway Bush on Plans for Iraq," *New York Times,* February 19, 2003. The estimate of February 15 protesters in the United States was obtained by consolidating data from Dominique Reynié, "Globalized Protest: Demonstrating in the Age of Globalization: The Case of Rallies against the Iraq War in 2003," https://www.academia.edu/6081355/GLOBALIZED_PROTEST._DEMONSTRATING_IN_THE_AGE_OF_GLOBALIZATION_THE_CASE_OF_RALLIES_AGAINST_THE_IRAQ_WAR_IN_2003_1; and Joris Verhulst, "February 15, 2003: The World Says No to War," in *The World Says No to War: Demonstrations against the War in Iraq,* ed. Stefaan Walgrave and Dieter Rucht (Minneapolis: University of Minnesota Press, 2010), 17. On Nixon's silent majority speech and the Vietnam antiwar movement, see Jeremy Varon, *Bringing the War Home: The Weather Underground, the Red Army Faction, and Revolutionary Violence in the Sixties and Seventies* (Berkeley and Los Angeles: University of California Press, 2004), 132–41. On the Mayday 1971 actions, see Lucy G. Barber, *Marching on Washington,* 179–218; L.A. Kauffman, *Direct Action,* 1–34.

54. On the notion of threat signaling through protest, see Zeynep Tufekci, *Twitter and Tear Gas,* 189–222.

55. Tom Wells, *The War Within,* 425–45 (the *Washington Post* is quoted on p. 425). Nancy Zaroulis and Gerald Sullivan, *Who Spoke Up?,* 324–28.

SELECTED BIBLIOGRAPHY AND RECOMMENDED READING

Anderson, Carol. *White Rage: The Unspoken Truth of Our Racial Divide.* New York: Bloomsbury USA, 2016.

Barber, Lucy G. *Marching on Washington: The Forging of an American Political Tradition.* Berkeley and Los Angeles: University of California Press, 2002.

Bond, Becky, and Zack Exley. *Rules for Revolutionaries: How Big Organizing Can Change Everything.* White River Junction, VT: Chelsea Green, 2016.

Boyd, Andrew, ed. *Beautiful Trouble: A Toolbox for Revolution.* New York: OR Books, 2012.

Branch, Taylor. *Parting the Waters: America in the King Years 1954–1963.* New York: Simon and Schuster, 1988.

Brown, Adrienne Maree. *Emergent Strategy: Shaping Change, Changing Worlds.* Chico, CA: AK Press, 2017.

Brown, Cynthia Stokes. *Ready from Within: Septima Clark and the Civil Rights Movement.* Trenton: Africa World Press, 1990.

Chenoweth, Erica, and Maria J. Stephan. *Why Civil Resistance Works: The Strategic Logic of Nonviolent Conflict.* New York: Columbia University Press, 2011.

Collier-Thomas, Bettye, and V.P. Franklin, eds. *Sisters in the Struggle: African American Women in the Civil Rights—Black Power Movement*. New York: New York University Press, 2001.

Crawford, Vicki L., Jacqueline Anne Rouse, and Barbara Woods, eds. *Women in the Civil Rights Movement: Trailblazers and Torchbearers, 1941–1965*. Bloomington and Indianapolis: Indiana University Press, 1993.

D'Emilio, John. *Lost Prophet: The Life and Times of Bayard Rustin*. New York: Free Press, 2003.

Dixon, Chris. *Another Politics: Talking across Today's Transformative Movements*. Oakland: University of California Press, 2014.

Engler, Mark, and Paul Engler. *This Is an Uprising: How Nonviolent Revolt Is Shaping the Twenty-First Century*. New York: Nation Books, 2016.

Euchner, Charles. *Nobody Turn Me Around: A People's History of the 1963 March on Washington*. Boston: Beacon, 2010.

Garfinkel, Herbert. *When Negroes March: The March on Washington Movement in the Organizational Politics for FEPC*. New York: Atheneum, 1968.

Gentile, Thomas. *March on Washington: August 28, 1963*. Washington, DC: New Day, 1983.

Gordon, Linda. *The Second Coming of the KKK: The Ku Klux Klan of the 1920s and the American Political Tradition*. New York: Liveright, 2017.

INCITE!, ed. *The Revolution Will Not Be Funded: Beyond the Non-Profit Industrial Complex*. Durham, NC: Duke University Press, 2017.

Isserman, Maurice. *If I Had a Hammer: The Death of the Old Left and the Birth of the New Left*. New York: Basic Books, 1987.

Jones, William P. *The March on Washington: Jobs, Freedom, and the Forgotten History of Civil Rights*. New York: W.W. Norton, 2013.

Kauffman, L.A. *Direct Action: Protest and the Reinvention of American Radicalism*. New York: Verso, 2017.

Kersten, Andrew E., and Clarence Lang. *Reframing Randolph: Labor, Black Freedom, and the Legacies of A. Philip Randolph*. New York: New York University Press, 2015.

Lucander, David. *Winning the War for Democracy: The March on Washington Movement, 1941–1946*. Urbana: University of Illinois Press, 2014.

McGirr, Lisa. *Suburban Warriors: The Origins of the New American Right*. Princeton, NJ: Princeton University Press, 2001.

McRae, Elizabeth Gillespie. *Mothers of Massive Resistance: White Women and the Politics of White Supremacy.* Oxford: Oxford University Press, 2018.

Meier, August, and Elliott Rudwick. *CORE: A Study in the Civil Rights Movement 1942–1968.* Urbana and Chicago: University of Illinois Press, 1975.

Payne, Charles M. *I've Got the Light of Freedom: The Organizing Tradition and the Mississippi Freedom Struggle.* Berkeley and Los Angeles: University of California Press, 1995.

Piven, Frances Fox. *Challenging Authority: How Ordinary People Change America.* Lanham, MD: Rowman and Littlefield, 2006.

Ransby, Barbara. *Ella Baker and the Black Freedom Movement: A Radical Democratic Vision.* Chapel Hill: University of North Carolina Press, 2003.

Robinson, Jo Ann Gibson. *The Montgomery Bus Boycott and the Women Who Started It.* Knoxville: University of Tennessee Press, 1987.

Robnett, Belinda. *How Long? How Long? African-American Women in the Struggle for Civil Rights.* New York: Oxford University Press, 1997.

Scanlon, Jennifer. *Until There Is Justice: The Life of Anna Arnold Hedgeman.* New York: Oxford University Press, 2016.

Skocpol, Theda. *Diminished Democracy: From Membership to Management in American Civic Life.* Norman: University of Oklahoma Press, 2003.

Skocpol, Theda, and Vanessa Williamson. *The Tea Party and the Remaking of Republican Conservatism.* Oxford: Oxford University Press, 2012.

Smucker, Jonathan Matthew. *Hegemony How-To: A Roadmap for Radicals.* Chico, CA: AK Press, 2017.

Solnit, Rebecca. *Hope in the Dark: Untold Histories, Wild Possibilities.* Chicago: Haymarket Books, 2016.

Sugrue, Thomas J. *Sweet Land of Liberty: The Forgotten Struggle for Civil Rights in the North.* New York: Random House, 2008.

Taylor, Keeanga-Yamahtta, ed. *How We Get Free: Black Feminism and the Combahee River Collective.* Chicago: Haymarket Books, 2017.

Theoharis, Jeanne. *A More Beautiful and Terrible History: The Uses and Misuses of Civil Rights History.* Boston: Beacon, 2018.

Theoharis, Jeanne, and Komozi Woodard, eds. *Freedom North: Black Freedom Struggles Outside the South, 1940–1980.* New York: Palgrave Macmillan, 2003.

———. *Groundwork: Local Black Freedom Movements in America.* New York: New York University Press, 2005.

Tufekci, Zeynep. *Twitter and Tear Gas: The Power and Fragility of Networked Protest.* New Haven, CT: Yale University Press, 2017.

Wells, Tom. *The War Within: America's Battle over Vietnam.* New York: Henry Holt, 1994.

Women's March Organizers and Condé Nast. *Together We Rise: Behind the Scenes at the Protest Heard around the World.* New York: Dey Street, 2018.

Zaroulis, Nancy, and Gerald Sullivan. *Who Spoke Up? American Protest against the War in Vietnam, 1963–1975.* Garden City, NY: Doubleday, 1984.

Zepeda-Millán, Chris. *Latino Mass Mobilization: Immigration, Racialization, and Activism.* Cambridge and New York: Cambridge University Press, 2017.

PHOTO CREDITS

Page ix   March on Washington fills Constitution Avenue: courtesy the Library of Congress, LC-DIG-ppmsca-08110

Page xi   2017 Women's March: Mario Tama, Getty Images

Page 7   Volunteers stack signs: courtesy the Library of Congress, LC-DIG-ppmsca-35530

Page 9   Women's Suffrage Parade: courtesy the Library of Congress, LC-USZ61–1154

Page 10   Ku Klux Klan procession: courtesy the Library of Congress, LC-DIG-hec-34203

Page 12   Bonus Army marchers: Portland *Oregonian*

Page 14   White House visit: courtesy the John F. Kennedy Presidential Library and Museum

Page 17   Picket at Southside Sundry: courtesy Special Collections and Archives, VCU Libraries

Page 18   Jones Beach protest: Associated Press

Page 19   CORE sit-in: courtesy the *Los Angeles Times* Photographic Archives, Collection 1429. Library Special Collections, Charles E. Young Research Library, UCLA

Page 21   Gwynn Oak Amusement Park: Walter McCardell, *Baltimore Sun*

Page 23   Organizer Bayard Rustin: courtesy the Library of Congress, LC-USZ62–133399

Page 24   St. Louis sit-in: Associated Press

Page 27   Detroit Walk to Freedom: Associated Press

Page 28   Volunteers prepare signs: courtesy the Library of Congress, LC-USZ62–135792

Page 31   Randolph, Wilkins, and Hedgeman: courtesy the Library of Congress, LC-DIG-ppmsca-35539

Page 32   Septima Clark: *California Eagle,* courtesy the Southern California Library

Page 35   Administrative and clerical staff: Werner Wolff, courtesy the Library of Congress, LC-DIG-ds-04559

Page 39   Joining in song: Leonard Freed, courtesy the Library of Congress, LC-DIG-ppmsca-35513

Page 40   Unauthorized sign: Marion K. Trikosko, courtesy the Library of Congress, LC-DIG-ppmsca-37230

Page 43   Lining up the leaders: courtesy the Library of Congress, LC-DIG-ppmsca-35521

Page 44   The march in progress: Warren K. Leffler, courtesy the Library of Congress, LC-DIG-ppmsca-03128

Page 45   The Fifth Avenue Peace Parade: Committee for Nonviolent Action—New England Records, courtesy Swarthmore College Peace Collection

Page 46   November 1965 antiwar protest: Theodore B. Hetzel, Theodore Brinton Hetzel Collection [CDG-A], courtesy Swarthmore College Peace Collection

Page 49   The 2004 March for Women's Lives: Susan Walsh, Associated Press

Page 51   Human Rights Campaign signs: Howard Sachs, Getty Images

Page 54   Protester locked to crane: Associated Press

Page 55   Blocking police car: Robert Larouche/*St. Louis Post-Dispatch*/Polaris

Page 57   Aftermath of the 1963 march: Leonard Freed, courtesy the Library of Congress

Page 58   2017 Women's March, New York: Carolina Kroon

Page 61   2017 Women's March, Kodiak, AK: Judy Heller

Page 62   2017 Women's March, Madison: Paul McMahon

Page 65   2017 Women's March, Los Angeles: Brendan Buckley

Page 66   2017 Women's March, St. Louis: Carrie Zukoski

Page 71   Women's March organizers meet: Kisha Bari

Page 75   The 1995 Million Man March: Maureen Keating, courtesy the Library of Congress, LC-DIG-ppmsca-38892

Page 83   Corralled on February 15, 2003: Garth Liebhaber

Page 85   The 1979 Lesbian and Gay March: Bettye Lane, courtesy the Lesbian Herstory Archives

Page 96   Muslim ban protest begins: L.A. Kauffman

Page 99   Muslim ban protest at JFK: Lucky Tran

Page 103   Protestors outraged by the US invasion of Cambodia: Ken Love, Bradford Lyttle Papers, courtesy Swarthmore Peace Collection

Page 105   Signs from the 2017 Women's March: Barbara Zaragoza

INDEX

2016 United States Election, legitimacy of, 74, 104

abortion rights, 48, 80
ACLU (American Civil Liberties Union), 65
ACORN (Association of Community Organizations for Reform Now), 50, 121n25
ACT UP (AIDS Coalition to Unleash Power), 47, 72, 121n24
AFL-CIO, 80
AIDS activism, 47, 72, 121n24
Al-Ghadban, Najeebah, 64, 123n32
anti-pipeline movement, 4, 64, 93
Arab Spring, 100

art-directed activism, 100
Awawdeh, Murad, 97, 127n51

Baker, Ella, 30, 72
Belafonte, Harry, 35, 68
Big Six, the, 11
Birmingham (Alabama), 13, 18, 21
Black Lives Matter, 64, 73, 82, 100
Black male empowerment, 34, 77, 78
Black Power, 22, 54, 115n2, 117n8, 120n17
Bland, Bob, 67, 123n34
Blockade of the World Trade Organization (1990), 82, 84, 102
blockades, 3, 82, 84, 102, 104
Bonus Army. *See* WWI Veterans, protests of

Brown, Michael, 100
Bush, George W., 4, 79–81, 101, 127n53

Cagan, Leslie, 84, 86, 110–11, 125n44, 126n45
canvassing, 93, 107
Capitol Grounds Act of 1882, 23
Chakraborty, Mrinalini, 67, 69, 110, 123n34, 124n37
Chenoweth, Erica, 100, 101, 122n30, 127n52
civil disobedience, 13, 22, 29, 33, 84, 102, 105
Civil Rights Act, 5
Clark, Septima, 30, 32 *fig.*, 33, 72, 90, 119n15
climate justice, 63, 82
Clinton, William Jefferson, 87
collective action, 1, 8–9, 37, 50, 72, 84, 88, 95, 104, 106
Combahee River Collective, 73, 124n38
communism, 11, 30, 47
Connor, Eugene "Bull," 13
CORE (Congress of Racial Equality), 11, 13, 19 *fig.*, 22, 26, 29, 52–54, 116n4, 117n7, 122n28
corporate globalization, 73, 82, 87
Crowd Counting Consortium, 114, 122n30

Detroit Walk to Freedom (1963), 9, 26–27 *fig.*, 115n2
direct action, 11, 19, 20, 29, 47, 53, 82, 84, 102, 105, 112, 124n38, 127n53

elected representatives, direct appeal to, 4, 106
Ellipse, the, 105

environmentalism. *See* climate justice
Equal Rights Amendment, 60, 80, 109, 121n23
Evers, Medgar, 15, 40 *fig.*

Facebook, 64, 67, 123n32, 124n40
Fairey, Shepard, 65
Farmer, James, 53–54, 116n4, 118n10, 122n28
Farrakhan, Louis, 76
feminism, 4, 34, 60, 63–64, 69, 72–73, 76, 88, 106, 124n36, 124n38
Ferguson (Missouri), 100
Fifth Avenue Peace Parade (1965), 45 *fig.*, 46, 120n23
Foner, Moe, 26, 118n11
football field, protests on, 3

Gathering for Justice, 68
Gentile, Thomas, 22, 116n4, 116n7, 117n8, 120n21, 121n26
Gorbachev, Mikhail, 80
Gottlieb, Sanford, 47
grassroots: broad progressivism in, 63; civil rights movement and, 22, 29, 30, 33, 36, 52; demobilization of local groups in, 53, 56; electoral work and, 93; empowerment and, 33, 72; energy from, 22, 29, 41, 89; female organizers and, 33, 36, 63, 72, 94; militancy in, 22; New Left and, 29; spontaneity and, 63; Tea Party and, 89, 92; white women and, 92–94
Greenberg, Leah, 92, 126n48

Hedgeman, Anna Arnold, 31 *fig.*, 32–34, 118n14

Height, Dorothy I., 34, 119n15

Hoover, Herbert, 8

Horowitz, Rachelle, 30, 36, 51–52, 118n13, 120n18, 121n26

Human Rights Campaign Fund, 51 *fig.*

identity politics, 63, 87

immigrant rights, 63, 73, 77, 79 *table*, 91 *table*, 93, 97–98, 121n23, 125n41

Indivisible, 92–93, 125n41, 126n48

Ingram, Janaye, 73, 110, 124n29, 124n38

intersectionalism, 63, 69, 73, 94, 124n36, 124n38, 124n39

Iraq War, 4, 78, 82, 84, 97, 101, 102, 109, 127n53

John Birch Society, 94

Kahn, Tom, 15–16, 30, 116n5, 118n13

Kennedy, John F., 13–15, 22–24, 41, 56, 81–82, 116n4

Kennedy, Robert F., 14 *fig.*

Kent State, 77, 104, 122n30

King, Bernice, 68

King, Coretta Scott, 34, 38, 119n16, 120n21

King, Martin Luther, Jr., 3, 14 *fig.*, 34, 35–38, 56, 68, 72, 90, 116n4, 118n10

Koch, Charles and David, 89

Ku Klux Klan, 8, 10 *fig.*, 94, 126n50

leafleting, 35–36, 52

Leninism, 30

LGBTQ movement, 2, 51*fig.*, 60, 63, 73, 76, 77 *table*, 84, 85 *fig.*, 87, 88, 100

local action, insufficiency of, 20, 26, 53, 116n7, 126n47

Magic Marker, invention of, 26, 118n10

Malcolm X, 29, 118n12

Mallory, Tamika, 68, 71 *fig.*

manhood rights, 34

March and Rally for Peace and Disarmament (1982), 79 *table*

March for Our Lives (2018), 91 *table*

March for Soviet Jewry (1987), 77 *table*

March for Women's Lives: in 1986, 77 *table;* in 1989, 77 *table;* in 1992, 77 *table,* 79 *table;* in 2004, 48, 49 *fig.*, 60, 77 *table,* 79 *table*

March on Washington for Jobs and Freedom (1963): Big Ten in, 11, 35, 37, 41; King's speech in, 3, 37–38; leadership in, 11, 30–37, 40–41; messaging in, 7, 25–27, 38; mobilization in, 76, 77 *table*; posters in, 7, 25–29, 38; right to vote in, 38; sexism in, 30–35, 48

March on Washington for Lesbian, Gay, and Bi Equal Rights and Liberation (1993), 51 *fig.*, 60, 76, 77 *table,* 79 *table*

March to End the War in Iraq, 77 *table*

mass marches, 3, 55, 80, 84, 86–87

Mayday 1971, 102, 127n53

Mendoza, Paola, 68

Millennium March for Equality (2000), 77 *table*

Million Man March (1995), 60, 74 *fig.*, 75 *fig.*, 76, 77 *table,* 78, 79 *table,* 125n1

Million Mom March (2000), 77 *table*

Moratorium to End the War in Vietnam, 90, 91 *table*

Morsell, John, 27, 33, 41, 118n11, 118n14, 119n14

Muslim ban (Executive Order 137969), 96 *fig.*, 97, 98, 99 *fig.*, 127n51

NAACP (National Association for the Advancement of Colored People), 13, 14 *fig.*, 15–16, 22, 26–27, 31 *fig.*, 33, 40 *fig.*, 41, 43 *fig.*, 52–53, 115n3, 118n11, 118n14

NALC (Negro American Labor Council), 11

NARAL (National Abortion Rights Action League), 48

Nation of Islam, 29, 76

National Action Network, 68

National Coming Out Day, 88

National Council of Churches, 31 *fig.*, 32

National Council of Negro Women, 33, 34

National Guard, 22, 104

National March on Washington for Lesbian and Gay Rights, 76, 77 *table*, 79 *table*, 84, 85 *fig.*, 88

National Mobilization to End the War, 77 *table*

National Urban League, 13

Nationwide Student Strike against the War, 91 *table*, 122n30

Native American Resistance, 64, 73

New Left, 29, 46, 106, 118n13

New York City Police Department, 54 *fig.*, 82, 100, 114

New York Immigration Coalition, 97

Nixon, Richard, 101, 104, 113, 122n30, 127n53

November 1965 antiwar protest, 46 *fig.*, 47, 121n23

NOW (National Organization of Women), 48–50

NYC Light Brigade, 98

Obama, Barack, 64–65, 87, 89, 92, 94

Occupy movement, 73, 82

Old Left, 30, 118n13

Pantsuit Nation, 67

Parks, Rosa, 36, 119n17

Payne, Charles, 36, 119n15, 120n17

Perez, Carmen, 68, 71 *fig.*

pickets, 55, 118n11

Planned Parenthood, 48, 65

Poitier, Sidney, 35

police departments: brutality in, 4, 13, 100, 106; crowd estimates and, 113–14; demonstrations against, 117n7; deployed against protest, 8, 13, 20, 21 *fig.*, 25, 54 *fig.*, 55–56, 106, 116n6; permit obstruction in, 82, 116n5, 118n10; as protest participants, 27

political buttons, as expression, 47

progressivism, 63–64, 106, 107

Protest of Cambodia Invasion, 78 *table*, 103 *fig.*, 104, 122n30

protest posters, 4–7, 22–29, 34, 37, 45, 47–52, 56, 63–66, 88–90, 97, 98, 103, 105 *fig.*, 110, 118n11, 123n32, 126n35

protests: as collective action, 1, 8–9, 37, 50, 72, 84, 95, 104; efficacy of, 1–5, 106; improvisation in, 10, 69, 102; mobilization in, 4, 8, 9, 11–12, 26, 35, 36, 37, 44–45, 47, 50–53, 64–66, 69, 76, 78–81, 84–95, 102–4, 109, 113, 119n17, 121n23, 122n27, 126n45; organizational structures in, 3–7; as power gathering, 1–5, 18, 30, 34, 50–51, 63, 81–84; women-led, 4, 63, 106

Pruitt, James Lee, 38, 120n20

public sympathy, 3

racial justice, 5, 8, 11, 14, 16, 18–22, 29, 30, 33–34, 44, 53–58, 63, 67–68, 81, 116n7

Randolph, Philip A., 8, 11–14, 14 *fig.*, 15–16, 25, 31 *fig.*, 32–34, 42 *fig.*, 68, 81, 116n4, 117n9, 118n10, 119n16, 120n18, 122n29

Reagan, Ronald, 80, 81

reproductive rights, 48, 60, 65, 77 *table*, 79 *table*, 80

Richardson, Gloria, 22, 117n8

right to public assembly, 82

riots, 2, 15–16, 21, 99, 100, 117n8

Robinson, Cleveland, 30, 117n10

Roosevelt, Franklin Delano, 8, 81

Rustin, Bayard, 12–16, 22, 23 *fig.*, 25, 30, 34, 36–37, 72, 81, 116n5, 117nn9–10, 118n11, 120n19

same-sex marriage, 87

SANE (National Committee for a Sane Nuclear Policy), 47, 121n23

Sarsour, Linda, 68, 71

SCLC (Southern Christian Leadership Conference), 13, 22, 30

Scott, James C., 2

SDS (Students for a Democratic Society), 29–30

Seattle, Washington, 82, 84, 102

Second National March on Washington for Gay and Lesbian Rights (1987), 77 *table*, 79 *table*

segregated lunch counters, 20

SEIU (Service Employees International Union), 65

Sharpton, Al, 68

Shook, Teresa, 67

Signal (app), 74

silent majority. *See* Nixon, Richard

silent vigils, 3

sit-ins, 19, 19 *fig.*, 20, 21 *fig.*, 24 *fig.* 63, 84, 103 *fig.*, 106, 117n7

SNCC (Student Nonviolent Coordinating Committee), 11, 13, 22, 29, 30, 41, 53

socialism, 30. *See also* YPSL

Solidarity Day, 77 *table*, 80

St. Louis (Missouri), 55 *fig.*, 56, 60, 66 *fig.*, 117n7, 122n28

Standing Rock, 64

stationary rallies, 82, 105

Stephan, Maria, 100, 101, 127n52

Stonewall riots, 2, 100

Stop the War Now, 46

Student Walkouts on Gun Violence, 91 *table*

Suffrage Procession and Pageant (1913), 8–9, 9 *fig.*

Tax Day Rallies, 89

Tea Party, 89–94, 126n46

Thelwell, Michael, 41, 53, 120n20, 120n22, 122n28

Theoharis, Jeanne, 6, 115nn1–2, 119n16, 120n21

Trump, Donald J., 4, 59, 61, 63, 67, 74, 87–90, 94, 97, 106, 114, 122nn31–32, 125n41

UAW (United Auto Workers Union), 11

UNITE HERE, 65

United for Peace and Justice, 90, 110, 126n47
uprisings, 81, 98, 100, 102, 122n27

Vietnam War, 45 *fig.*, 46, 76, 77 *table*, 80, 102, 104, 113
Vietnam War Out Now Rally, 77 *table*
violence against civil disobedience: assassination in, 4, 15, 100; backlash in, 20; fire hoses in, 13; lynching in, 15; police dogs in, 13, 15; state sanction in, 2, 8, 13, 20, 21 *fig.*, 25, 54 *fig.*, 55, 56, 100, 106, 116n6

Wallace, George, 30
Webster v. Reproductive Health, 80
Wilkins, Roy, 14 *fig.*, 16, 31 *fig.*, 41 *fig.*, 115n3, 118n10, 119n14

Women's Marches (2017), 4, 45, 59–73, 61 *fig.*, 62 *fig.*, 63, 65 *fig.*, 66 *fig.*, 71 *fig.*, 77 *table*, 79, 88, 90 91 *table*, 92–94, 97–98, 100, 102, 105 *fig.*, 110, 122n30, 122n34, 123n32, 124nn36–39, 126n48, xi *fig.*; grassroots mobilization in, 69–70, 89; intersectionalism in, 94, 124n36; leadership in, 67–68, 123n34; social media in, 64, 67, 98; Unity Principles in, 73, 124n39
Women's Marches (2018), 91 *table*
World Says No to Bush Agenda at the RNC (2004), 79 *table*
"World Says No to War" protests (2003), 84, 91 *table*
WWI Veterans, protests of, 8, 12 *fig.*

YPSL (Young People's Socialist League), 30, 118n13